The Land and People of
NEW ZEALAND

Hei-Tiki

PORTRAITS OF THE NATIONS SERIES

The Land and People of
NEW ZEALAND

Edna Mason Kaula

J. B. LIPPINCOTT COMPANY

PHILADELPHIA AND NEW YORK

FOR

Robin Allison Kaula

PHOTOGRAPHIC CREDITS

Grateful acknowledgment is made to the following sources for pictures on pages noted: New Zealand Embassy, 10, 23, 26, 32, 36, 44, 46, 56, 63, 72, 81, 87, 92, 97, 100, 103, 119, 121, 122, 130, 155; New Zealand Consulate General, 12, 16, 28, 34, 107, 109, 113, 132, 143.

The author also gratefully acknowledges the generous assistance of members of the staff of the New Zealand Consulate General in gathering material and checking data in connection with the preparation of this book.

Map and illustration by the author.

Contents

PORTRAITS OF THE NATIONS SERIES

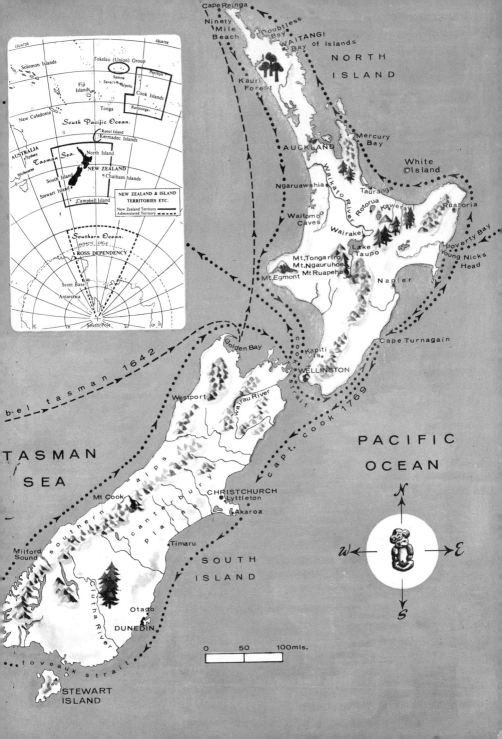

1

Land of the Long White Cloud

DAY AFTER DAY Kupe's and Ngahue's canoes rode the high Pacific Ocean waves southwestward from their mythical homeland, Hawaiki. Though weak from hunger and parched from thirst, the two Polynesian navigators, with their crews, were filled with hope. Frigate birds and terns soared above them; they swooped about the battered crafts or dived for fish. Their presence indicated that land lay not too far ahead. Kupe shaded his eyes as he strained forward and scanned the horizon. Among the scudding clouds one hung motionless. Kupe fixed his attention on the long white cloud until, suddenly, he gave a great shout of joy and relief:

"*Aotearoa!*" he cried, meaning Land of the Long White Cloud. The crew members saw that mountaintops pierced the cloud and that a rich green shore line showed below it. As they paddled closer they heard a gentle surf coming in to a broad white beach. Kupe was the first Maori known to reach New Zealand shores; the land he discovered more than one thousand years ago is still called Aotearoa by many New Zealanders. Maori is the Polynesian word for native; it was the name adopted by those Polynesians who settled in New Zealand so long ago that they have come to be thought of as indigenes.

New Zealand, the most remote and loneliest member of the British Commonwealth of Nations, breaks the surface of the Pacific Ocean between the thirty-fourth and forty-eighth latitudes south. The Tasman Sea, one of the stormiest bodies of water in the world, lies to the west; it separates New Zealand from Australia, her nearest neighbor, by nearly 1300 miles. To the south spread the bleak waters of the Ross Sea and Antarctica,

Arrival of the Maoris in New Zealand.

COURTESY OF THE AUCKLAND ART GALLERY

while only a few islands dot the rolling Pacific Ocean between New Zealand and South America.

Two million years ago, in the Cenozoic Era, New Zealand was already isolated, for fossil remains have been found of creatures which, even in past ages, were unique to New Zealand. One theory is that New Zealand was, at one time, connected with South America by a land bridge. Even earlier New Zealand was studded with volcanoes, all but three of which are now extinct.

The mainland of New Zealand consists of three islands—the North Island, the South Island, and a smaller one, Stewart Island. These three islands stretch north and south for one thousand miles. The country's total area is 103,500 square miles, slightly less than that of the state of Colorado. Nowhere is New Zealand wider than 280 miles, yet compact within this area lie all types of landscape and many features found nowhere but in New Zealand.

New Zealand's subtropical north consists of a narrow peninsula penetrating far into the warm Pacific Ocean and ending in high cliffs called Cape Reinga and North Cape. From the eastern shore of this long finger of land fine, blazing white sand is carried away from dunes for glassmaking. The Ninety-Mile Beach —which is closer to sixty than ninety miles in length—stretches along the western shore. Unlike the eastern beaches, the sand where the Tasman Sea pounds is gray in color. The prevailing west winds build up sandbanks so that beach contours change from season to season and driftwood, brought down by rivers in floodtime, strews the beaches.

Between the east and west shores stand the dense kauri pine forests. Some of these ancient timber giants are three thousand

Cape Reinga, the northernmost tip of New Zealand.

years old. They rise from a labyrinth of twisting vines, ferns, shrubs, gorgeous orchids, and other parasitic and perching plants. A cloisterlike calm hangs over the kauri forests; aromatic plants exude a refreshing, earthy fragrance.

Farther south the land thickens. At a dozen points along the coast deep indentations bring the sea flowing inland. South of a five-mile-wide isthmus, which is straddled by the northern city of Auckland, the land broadens into rich pastureland. The climate is balmy, the rainfall adequate, the livestock roaming through the hills are sleek and fat. Nearby, a river flows through deep, underground caves that are lit by the cold blue light from glowworms. Another river, the Waikato, New Zealand's longest, empties into the Tasman Sea after meandering for 220 miles across this peaceful landscape.

The volcanic plateau is where the Waikato River rises on Mount Ruapehu, flows into and out from Lake Taupo, then through narrow gorges as rapids and cascades. Centered in the thermal regions, Lake Taupo, 238 square miles in area, is New Zealand's largest lake. It is 25 miles long, 17 miles wide, and 1200 feet above sea level. Overlooking the lake are Ruapehu, Ngauruhoe, and Tongariro, three magnificent volcanic mountains, and between the lake and the north coast hot pools and geysers bubble and roar.

Near the west coast, in the moist Taranaki region, one solitary extinct volcano, Mount Egmont, dominates the green countryside. Mount Egmont, 8260 feet in height, is snow-crowned and, in symmetrical beauty, resembles Japan's Mount Fuji.

The North Island's east coast region combines sheep farms with orchards and market gardens. It is strung with shell-strewn beaches though in places impenetrable woodlands extend along the shore line. Eastland terminates in the North Island's southern tip, close to a harbor ringed about by steep hills where New Zealand's capital, Wellington, is located.

Cook Strait, about twenty miles at its narrowest point, separates New Zealand's North and South Islands. It interrupts a central mountain spine that divides New Zealand from the North Island's center clear down to the southernmost point of the South Island. In the north high mountains alternate with undulating hills and occasional plains, but in the South Island the Southern Alps climb higher and higher in a grand profusion of snow-capped peaks which culminate in Mount Cook at 12,349 feet. To the Maoris of New Zealand, Mount Cook is *Aorangi,* the Cloud Piercer. New Zealand has more than 220 named peaks of over 7500 feet and 17 peaks that exceed 10,000 feet in height. Others, in the wild, unexplored regions to the south, still wait to be surveyed and named. Glaciers are wedged between the high mountains. Tasman Glacier, extending for eighteen miles, is New Zealand's largest. This frozen river is also the largest glacier in a temperate zone. Almost half of the South Island is uncultivable because of the rugged nature of the Southern Alps, so nearly 3,000,000 acres of mountains, lakes, and sounds have been set aside as a National Reserve.

The South Island's coast line along Cook Strait is an intricate pattern of bays, inlets, and beaches with soft gold-colored sand. This region is envied for its mild climate and long hours of clear sunshine, but high mountains, which protect the area from wind, block easy access to other sections of the South Island.

By contrast the west coast has a high rainfall—150 inches annually. Westland is a narrow strip of plain enclosed in mountain ranges and the Tasman Sea. The mountains drop from 10,000 feet to sea level within twenty miles along the west coast. Sheep farming and orchards give way to timber cutting, gold and coal mining; an atmosphere of pioneer days prevails. Westland's one link with eastern regions is by railroad through a tunnel hewn beneath the Southern Alps for 5.25 miles. The train emerges from the tunnel onto a plateau in the High Country that has, for a background, snow fields and glaciers. Rivers fed by glacier water have cut deep gorges through the mountains as they flow toward lakes cradled among the peaks. These mountain lakes are among the loveliest in the world, for they are fringed with luxuriant trees, ferns, and flowers. The High Country is one of the few places in New Zealand with extremes i climate; sudden freezes make fire pots a necessity in every orchard. The rivers that rise in the Southern Alps and flow into the lakes find a way, eventually, across the Canterbury Plains and into the Pacific Ocean. The Canterbury region embraces the largest, richest plain in New Zealand where food crops and fat lambs flourish.

Gorse and broom cover the weathered hills in the south but toward the west coast sounds, or Fiordland, alternating hills and mountains rise beyond canyons, carved by rapid flowing rivers, until heavy forest is reached. This country is difficult to traverse but, for motorists, a tunnel has been blasted through the head of one valley.

Fiordland is broken by steep-sided inlets that have been scooped by glaciers and beaten smooth by penetrating seas. Milford Sound, where the water is one mile deep, is famous as a beauty spot. One of thirteen fiords, it extends inland for nine miles and is one mile wide. Locked serenely within Milford Sound's steep walls, vivid green shrubbery is broken by waterfalls and glistening patches of bare rock. Reflections in the water shimmer and send up shafts of clear sunrays from the glassy surface of the water, giving a great play of light and shade. Occasionally dolphins swim to the head of the fiord; their frolics make wide ripples and cause the reflected light to dance. Dominating this superb scene are two mountains, Mitre Peak (5560 feet high) and Mount Pembroke (6710 feet high). The Maoris gave the name of *Piopio Tahi* to Milford Sound, which means Rare Bird.

A miniature ocean liner, the motor ship *Wairu,* carries passengers across Foveaux Strait to Stewart Island where the varied beauties of the mainland continue. Although only 670 square

Half Moon Bay on Stewart Island.

miles in area, this small triangular-shaped island is packed with a profusion of rare trees, plants, a mountain, and shores that are forest-clad to the water's edge. Stewart Island is walled in by seas which, on stormy days, crash against the rocks in fountains of spray, keeping the island's 540 inhabitants weatherbound for days, but they are content to remain isolated, for they live mainly from the sea as fishermen. The sense of peace and remoteness draw many visitors, along with hundreds of thousands of birds which recognize Stewart Island as a natural bird sanctuary.

The surrounding seas prevent excessive summer heat or winter cold in New Zealand's three main islands. The average temperatures range from 59° Fahrenheit in the north to 49°F. in the south. Although the highest temperatures occur east of the mountain range, where it climbs to the nineties in the summer, the greatest extremes of heat and cold occur in the South Island. There, in the south center, 100°F. is not uncommon in the summertime and 20°F. for a few cold days in winter. The average rainfall is 13 inches a year, but over the Southern Alps it averages 300 inches. For most of New Zealand, however, rainfall averages between 25 and 60 inches. Rain comes as short, heavy downpours so that there is plenty of sunshine, of which six hours daily is the average.

The mountains and the country's isolation produce conditions that create winds. Although never of great strength, New Zealand's winds are insistent. They toss the surrounding seas and bend the forest trees in gusty sweeps. The most characteristic features of New Zealand's weather, however, are the quick changes. Rainfall, sunshine, and winds follow one another in abrupt succession throughout a single day.

New Zealanders observe a permanent half-hour daylight saving time. And when dwellers in the Northern Hemisphere look for snow, New Zealanders anticipate long hours of sunshine in their entrancing outdoors for, being located in the Southern Hemisphere, their seasons are the reverse of those in America and Europe; the summer months are November, December, and January.

Dependencies of New Zealand include the two groups that form the tropical Cook Islands, about 2000 miles northeast of

New Zealand's mainland. The seven islands that comprise the northern group and two of the southern are coral atolls, while the remaining six of the southern group are extinct volcanic cones. Altogether the Cook Islands are scattered over 850,000 square miles of ocean. Both northern and southern groups lie in the path of hurricanes which strike between December and March when the weather is humid. For the rest of the year the southern group enjoys mild and balmy weather. Rarotonga, in the south, is watered by streams from its rugged mountains, 2110 feet in height, but the other islands are dependent upon tanks for catching rain water. Cook Islanders are British subjects and New Zealand citizens. A New Zealand Resident Commissioner (advised by an executive council of eight members) presides over the Cook Islands Assembly. The islanders receive free medical, surgical, and dental treatment and free schooling —which is compulsory from six to sixteen years—all of which costs the New Zealand government about $65 a head for a population that numbers 18,000. About $1,215,000 worth of fruits, copra, and pearl shell were exported in 1958, but more than $2,500,000 worth of imports included oil, yard goods, motor vehicles and their parts. Although the New Zealand government maintains a shipping service, isolation from their markets and from one another is the major economic handicap of the Cook Islands.

Niue Island, 100 square miles in area, is 19 degrees south of the equator and 580 miles west of the Cook Islands. Its people also are British subjects and New Zealand citizens. They mill the timber from the island's forested center and export copra, bananas, kumaras (sweet potatoes), and plaited basketware.

The coral-reefed Tokelau group, between 8° and 10° south of the equator, are under control of New Zealand's Department of Island Territories. Nauru, a little island almost on the equator, supplies most of the phosphate rock used by New Zealanders in the manufacture of fertilizers. The island is jointly held as a United Nations trust by Great Britain, Australia, and New Zealand. Toward the south lie the Chatham Island group, 467 miles east of Lyttelton in the South Island. Because of its isolation, development of this group has been slow, but since 1949, when general administration was placed under the Department of Island Territories and a shipping service was started, trade has improved. Now the islanders export their sheep to the South Island, for sheep farming is their chief occupation.

The inhabitants of New Zealand's island dependencies are mostly Polynesians. They number about 25,000, plus an additional 8500 who have migrated to New Zealand's mainland because of more varied opportunities for advancement. Altogether New Zealand cares for two thirds of all the Pacific islands' Polynesian people.

In 1923 the New Zealand government undertook the administration of the uninhabited Ross Dependency, which is that part of Antarctica immediately south of New Zealand extending to the South Pole. It has been the scene of many antarctic explorations including various expeditions made by Admiral Byrd.

Thus New Zealand, with her dependencies, stretches from the equator to the South Pole, from the coral reefs of the South Pacific Ocean to the frozen wastes and the brilliant lights of Aurora Australis, and the three main islands in themselves are crammed with earth's beauties and wonders, giving them the justified title of "Nature's Sample Room."

2

/\.\/\.\/\.\/\.\/\.\

The People and Their Cities

LITTLE MORE than a hundred and twenty years ago the grand-parents and great-grandparents of most of today's New Zealanders of European origin sailed the 13,500 miles from Britain as pioneers. Sometimes the voyage took as long as eight months; many ships were lost at sea. But to those who survived the journey, the land they came to looked good; they were determined to remain and to prosper. The forests were free of dangerous animals, the climate was mild, fish and birds were abundant, the earth was rich. At first the settlers lived in daub and wattle huts; later they cut the tall timber for permanent homes. Yet for many years life was precarious and insecure, so they left the interior unexplored. The uncertainty of not knowing when fierce and resentful natives would attack them kept the early settlers clinging to the coasts in small colonies. There are Maoris living today whose great-grandfathers fought with courage and savagery, combined with an extraordinary chivalry, against the white invaders. Now the Maori and Pakeha—the Maori word for the white man—live in harmony. Of New Zealand's 2,500,000 inhabitants, 7% are Maoris and, if the present Maori growth continues, 13% of New Zealand children under fourteen will be Maoris by 1972. Their rate of increase is as high as, or higher than, that of any other people in the world.

There are a few descendants of French and Dalmatian settlers and, since World War II, 6000 Hollanders have come to New Zealand, but more than 90% of New Zealanders are of British stock. Although a total of 61,000 persons have settled in New Zealand under assisted immigration schemes since World War II, more than 48,000 of these new settlers came from the British Isles. Because New Zealand maintains a British way of life a preference will continue to be given to British settlers.

It is understandable that a New Zealander's outlook is still colored by Britain's when most of them have English surnames. Many New Zealanders mean England when they speak of "home," though among the present generation this habit is less frequent. Being far removed from the world's great centers has given New Zealanders a longing for travel, to visit Britain—home. And New Zealanders are found everywhere—as technicians in China, as surveyors in Jahore, as students in European universities, as climbers of challenging mountains, and as hikers all over Europe.

After more than a century of being a separate entity a recognizable New Zealand type has emerged. He is healthy, of average height, usually fair-haired, blue-eyed, and rugged of complexion. A New Zealander is lean but muscular; his appetite is tremendous. Statistics show that his average caloric intake every day is 3400. Compared with a United States citizen, a New Zealander consumes more cereal, potatoes, sugar, and almost twice as much milk, milk products, and meat—233 pounds a year for each person. A New Zealander's consumption of butter is four times that of an American. He needs energy foods for his strenuous outdoor activities and for his sports, to which he is passionately devoted. A New Zealander has enormous regard for individual sportsmanship, for fair play.

As a do-it-yourself man a New Zealander has no equal. This talent is particularly noticeable in his repairing of motor vehicles, of which there is one to every four persons. A New Zealander will undertake any job around the house from building a new wing to installing the plumbing. An opportunity to exercise this skill has come with a new fad, to own a weekend *bach* or *crib*—a small vacation house—by the seashore. Of course, a New Zealander builds the bach himself. Even women and girls have an all-round talent for fixing things. The girls in one high school recently were given a choice of continuing with cooking lessons or taking woodwork and 120 of 200 girls chose woodwork. They made Swedish-style chairs and settees the first term and, according to their instructor, were more adept at woodwork than the boys, though they lacked the same "constructional intelligence." Probably this remarkable ability to do it himself is inherited, for in the early days a settler not only cut the timber from virgin forest but, with the assistance of his wife and family, constructed his own crude home as well.

Today, whether it is a forest, woods, or scrubland, a New Zealander refers to it as the *bush*. Fields are *paddocks*, a small farmer is a *cocky,* and a sheep or cattle ranch is a *station.* The New Zealand dialect is a combination of Scots and south and north English and is pleasing to hear. There is very little variation in accent throughout the country except in the far south, a region settled by the Scots; there, if possible, the dialect is more Scottish than the Scots.

A New Zealander is shy and guarded when approached by a stranger; he is apt to be inarticulate, especially if the stranger brags or overstates, a trait regarded as a major fault. But should the stranger exhibit an interest in manual work the New Zealander will quickly unbend. A New Zealander is slow to give confidence and slower still to ask others to give theirs, but once his reserve is broken and his friendship won he is generous and hospitable to a very high degree. New Zealanders entertain in their homes, which they usually own. No matter at what time of day the visitor calls he will be given a cup of tea with sandwiches and homemade cake. And the first sound an overnight guest hears in the morning is the rattle of the teacups when he is brought an early morning "cuppa," as an eye opener, and a paper-thin slice of bread and butter.

Houses are always enclosed by fences but inside, between the front gate and the house, flowers and shrubs are made to grow to a size and quality unequaled anywhere, for all New Zealanders seem to have green thumbs. Competitions are held in every town and suburb, not only for outstanding blooms and arrangements, but for floral harmony in streets also.

It can be disconcerting to a stranger when he attends his first party in a home, for the men and women tend to separate. Unless he knows every person present a New Zealander's reserve again becomes evident. The women chat in one corner while the men, with heads together, discuss their baches or ball-games or, quite possibly, farming. Most New Zealanders know a great deal about cows and sheep, which seems strange indeed, for 65% of New Zealand's people live in the cities.

In towns and cities throughout New Zealand everyone observes the long weekend. Shops are closed on Saturday; no papers are published on Sunday. On Fridays, however, the shops remain open until 9 P.M. It is then that New Zealanders converge to do their marketing, keeping to the left if they drive to town, exchanging news and gossip and sharing tea with old friends, thus making Friday the friendliest night in the week.

A town attains city status when its population reaches 20,000. There are eighteen cities but four of them—Auckland, Wellington, Christchurch, and Dunedin—are by far the largest. Evenly spaced down the length of both islands, three are port cities. Christchurch alone lies inland seven miles from Lyttelton, its port.

Auckland, in the north with a subtropical climate, has 466,-300 inhabitants. It is a city built on seven extinct volcanoes; the biggest, Rangitoto, stands at the harbor entrance. Auckland

is also a city of water. One of its two harbors, Waitemata, carries more yachts and pleasure boats than any other city of its size in the world. A long bridge across Waitemata was completed in 1959, thus bringing the sprawling garden suburbs closer and making the beaches and play areas more available to those who live in the city. Auckland is a focus of maritime export and import rather than industry. Freighters, bound for world markets, take meat, wool, and dairy products from Auckland where more tonnage is handled than in any other New Zealand port. One view from the harbor is of the museum that is also a war memorial. The handsome building, which dominates the city from a hilltop, houses Maori antiquities including one war canoe, 82 feet long by 5 feet wide, capable of carrying 100 men. Auckland was once New Zealand's capital but in 1865 government was moved to the geographically centered city of Wellington.

The first view of Wellington, when approached by railroad, is when the train bursts from a tunnel, for New Zealand's capital is flanked by steep hills encircling a sparkling blue bowl of a harbor which, more often than not, is flecked with whitecaps. Much of the city is built on reclaimed land—the wooden houses, overlooking the business section, on ledges cut deep into slopes. A cable car ascends and descends one hill at an alarming angle providing access to suburbs that lie beyond the hills. But beside the city, homes built on the gentler slopes above a crescent-shaped cove create a French Riviera atmosphere. City expansion extends northward to a suburb called the Hutt that is a city in itself. The combined population of Wellington and the Hutt is 255,700.

Wellington's settlers, in 1840, first built across the harbor,

Auckland in 1852, an engraving from a painting by Patrick Joseph Hogan.

Cable car carries passengers high above Wellington and the harbor.

but the Cook Strait winds forced them to move their few buildings, on rafts, to the present site. Two years later a fire demolished the raupo-thatched cottages. The determined settlers rebuilt in clay and brick but an earthquake shook them down. When the settlers decided to abandon the project as a bad try and sail off to Australia, their ship was wrecked on one of the harbor's headlands. It is just as well that the settlers gave up attempts to leave, to stay instead and to rebuild in wood, for Wellington has grown to be a beautiful city. Now, with earthquake-proof concrete, Wellington is building upward with fine modern structures several stories high. And it can claim to be

New Zealand's most cosmopolitan city. Because it is the center of administration diplomats come to it from all over the world, encouraging the patronage of foreign restaurants, delicatessens, and specialty shops and fostering an interest in the arts. Wellington supports a National Orchestra, ballet and opera companies, and a library, the Turnbull, that houses a valuable collection of Pacific books, maps, and drawings. Wellington people, though still battling the winds and lacking the rolling countryside of other cities, find this compensation enough.

Sometimes the winds cause the ferry from Wellington to Lyttelton to pitch in the turbulent seas. An overnight trip brings the visitor across Cook Strait and halfway down the east coast of South Island to the port that belongs to Christchurch. This city of 226,800 inhabitants is one of the few in New Zealand that can extend itself indefinitely, for it lies on the Canterbury Plains. Town planners have made the most of this advantage. Unwavering streets extend for miles, broken only by the Avon River, which flows through the city beneath weeping willows brought from beside Napoleon Bonaparte's grave on St. Helena. And, on a towpath parallel to the river, university students relax while studying, for Christchurch, like New Zealand's other three main cities, has its university. By the Avon River, also, among imported English oaks and tall birches, stands a monument to the memory of Captain Robert Scott, the English explorer. In 1911, Captain Scott reached the South Pole but on the return journey he and his party perished in blizzards and $-40°F$. cold. Today, Christchurch is again the base for antarctic exploration; from there the United States Navy Deep Freeze expeditions make daily contact, by radio, with the men who are stationed in the polar regions, on picket ships and aircraft. The

Christchurch. (Left) *University students row on the Avon.*
(Right) *The heart of the city, Cathedral Square.*

Church of England cathedral, of Gothic design, stands in Christ-church's central square. Streets leading from the cathedral bear the names of English bishoprics; the squares are named for English martyr bishops. The level streets are crammed with bicycles and buses whose drivers extend an unusual courtesy to mothers with children. A driver not only helps a mother with her baby aboard but hangs the baby carriage on a hook attached to the front of the bus.

Two hundred and forty miles south of the "most English city outside England" stands Dunedin, the most Scottish. The Reverend Thomas Burns, nephew of the famous poet, was among the members of the Scottish Free Kirk who founded Dunedin. Today, Robert Burns's statue stands before the cathedral in the city's central square. Of seventy-six migrants' ships to sail from Scotland in 1848, seventy-three came to this southern port. Their passengers were austere, earnest folk who settled in an area as rugged as the one they had left. And they were civic-minded. Generous endowments made it possible for Dunedin to have the first university, the Pioneers' Museum, which contains the finest collection of Polynesian art in the world, and so many churches, all well attended, that Dunedin is sometimes called the city of churches. Dunedin was also the first city to have gaslight, piped water, electricity, cable cars for its steep hills, and trains. On special days parades move through Dunedin's streets led by Scottish clansmen in full regalia. Skirling bagpipes bring cheers from the crowds that stand before their stone and brick buildings, which are as numerous as wooden ones. The streets sweep down to a long, narrow harbor with a dredged channel that permits ocean liners to berth right beside the main business section.

Shipping brought prosperity to the city which continues to grow since refrigeration was invented. New Zealand, before then, was threatened with a devastating depression, but in 1882 the first shipment of frozen mutton set sail from Dunedin's harbor. It was the start of an industry that has made New Zealand the biggest exporter of frozen and chilled meat in the world. It comes as no surprise, then, that Dunedin's motto is "By Ships We Live."

3

/\\./\\./\\./\\./\\.\

A Land of Milk and Honey

IN A SEASON that lasts for three or four months the sight by day and the sound by night are the double-decker truckloads of fat lambs trundling over the roads to the freezing works. Every year more than 19,000,000 lambs and 6,500,000 sheep are brought to the 35 processing plants that operate close to export loading ports. Not only is New Zealand the world's largest exporter of meat, with lamb and mutton as the biggest items, but three quarters of the total amount exported by all countries comes from New Zealand. And of this amount over 80% goes to Britain. It is estimated that more than 48,500,000 sheep on 23,000 separate farms are supported on the three types of sheep farms in New Zealand.

High in the mountains, where the land is of an inferior quality, sheep are grown for their wool on huge holdings some-times 108,000 acres in area. The homesteads are isolated places where, in the off season, the station hands play ice hockey and other winter sports. But from September, the lambing sea-son, through November and December, the shearing months, these high lonely centers are the scenes of tremendous activity. Specially trained dogs assist the musterers in bringing in the sheep, which sometimes climb to inaccessible heights among the mountain peaks. Scouting planes spot sheep hidden behind rocky ridges or in the purple-shadowed ravines. Then the men move in to retrieve them. They climb steep and dangerous cliffs; they scale precipices until every sheep is brought to a lower level.

Gangs of shearers travel from station to station in the shear-ing season. By using power clippers skillful workers can remove an entire wool fleece intact. One shearer, Godfrey Bowen, es-tablished a world record by shearing 463 sheep in nine hours. He fills a vital role by demonstrating and teaching his technique to aspiring young shearers for, with New Zealand's rising sheep population, there is a shortage of shearers. Godfrey Bowen, now a champion shearer, was once an office worker. New Zea-land's wool-growing sheep are brought down to lower levels during the winter months but, like all livestock in New Zea-land's equable climate, they are left to graze in the open the year around.

The second type of farms are in New Zealand's hill coun-try. These support the breeding flocks which produce both fine wool and flavorful meat. With continuous research, by using every advantage science offers and in experimentation, sheep breeders have made New Zealand the second largest wool pro-

ducer and exporter in the world. Most breeding ewes are Romneys, with a few Merinos and Corriedales. The lambs they produce are fattened on low-lying pastures where New Zealand's third type of farms are located. Credit is given, also, to New Zealand's grasslands for the high quality of the country's products. In recent years aerial top dressing, seeding, and fertilizing have added materially to their richness. In a single year aircraft from various companies spread 428,000 tons of superphosphates over nearly 4,000,000 acres.

Sharing the rich pastures, where the grass grows throughout the year, are about 6,000,000 head of cattle. For the most part cattle are raised as a by-product of the sheep industry, but 2,000,000 cows on dairy farms produce enough milk to establish New Zealand as by far the biggest exporter of dairy products in the world. All but 10% of the herds, which are mostly Jersey cows, are located in the North Island. Farmers whose lands lie within sight of beautiful Mount Egmont in the Taranaki District claim that their lands are the richest in the world. The government Department of Agriculture and Scientific Research advises farmers constantly on improved methods of production so that on first-class farms the average yield of butterfat reaches higher than 450 pounds in a good season while the high over-all average is 285 pounds. Prize winners, of course, climb to the 600- to 800-pound bracket for butterfat production.

The factories that churn the sweet cream into 400,000,000 pounds of butter every year are nearly all co-operatives. They are owned by the farmers themselves. The butter and the 85,-000,000 pounds of cheese made in the factories pass rigid tests

(Above) *Merino sheep are eye-clipped and driven to grazing land on Glentanner Station in Canturbury.* (Below) *Moving to rich grazing grounds in Ruakituri Valley, North Island.*

THE NEW ZEALAND HERALD

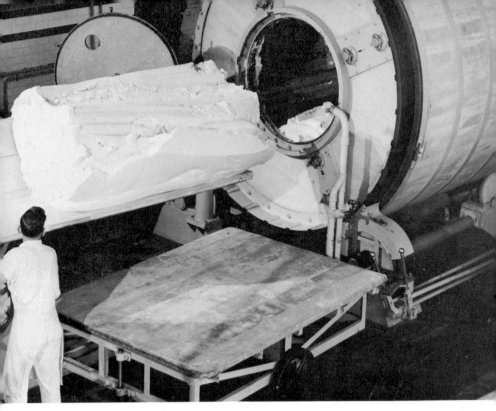

Please pass the butter! One ton of it being lowered from churn to trolley.

before being exported, mostly to Britain. Dried milk and casein are exported also from the co-operatives.

Veal is a by-product of the dairy farms. In the springtime plaintive moos come from newborn male calves that wait in enclosures outside each farm for the butcher's truck. One and a half million calves and 900,000 head of beef cattle are killed annually. By chilling beef for export, rather than freezing it, the texture and flavor are retained so that competition with suppliers nearer to Britain is made easier. Both the United States and Japan are remunerative markets, also, for the approximately 85,000 tons of frozen and chilled beef exported every year out of an estimated total production of 212,000 tons.

These three farm products—wool, meat, and dairy products —account for 90% of New Zealand's exports; they are the country's greatest source of income. But with its varied climate, New Zealand is also able to grow most kinds of fruits and vegetables. Thousands of commercial orchards flourish in both the North and the South Islands. New Zealanders, as a people, are fond of vegetables and most families grow enough to fill their own needs in trim gardens which also contain one or two fruit trees. Extensive clover pastures are pollinated by bees from apiaries, over 60% of which are situated in the North Island. In one record year 100 tons of beeswax and 6400 tons of surplus honey were harvested.

The rich yield from New Zealand's farms is closely supervised in its marketing. A government Marketing Commission takes over all butter and cheese intended for export; it regulates the marketing of these products and determines a guaranteed price to the farmers.

The meat producer is free to sell his stock as he thinks fit and most stock is bought by meat-packing companies. Wool buyers, from the world's important wool countries, attend auctions during the shearing season. Other authorities supervise the marketing of wool, fruits, vegetables, grains, and honey.

Thus New Zealand farmers are provided with an assurance of a greater stability of income as the producers of the abundance of food from the good land which is truly one flowing with milk and honey.

The First
Three Hundred Years

SHARING New Zealand's riches are the Maoris, who are but one branch of the many Polynesians who are widespread throughout the Pacific islands. Physically taller than the average European, they are also broad in the shoulders and heavy-limbed. However, in proportion to their height the Maoris' legs are shorter. A Maori's hair is black and wavy above a complexion that compares with a good sun tan. His nose is flat, his nostrils widespread, and his brown eyes are keen, for he has excellent eyesight as well as acute hearing. His teeth, when a Maori smiles, gleam white and evenly and, according to the experts, are the finest in the world. By nature a Maori is full of fun and given to practical joking. At the same time his bearing is dignified, for he possesses innate good manners. He is men-

36

Ancient Maori rivercraft and traditional costumes are features of ceremonies commemorating an earlier way of life.

PHOTO BY W. HALL RAINE

tally alert and in the early days was quick to experiment and to learn new skills.

The Maori language, a dialect of the Polynesian, is comprised of the five vowels and eight consonants. The vowels are pronounced thus: A as in *father,* E, as in *ten,* I as in *seen,* O as in *border* and U as in *moon.* The consonants are H, K, M, N, P, R, T, W, and NG- a nasal sound pronounced softly as in *wringer,* never as in *finger.* No two consonants come together in a word except WH, sounded softly as in *where.* Every syllable ends in a vowel and every vowel is sounded with equal emphasis. For instance, *Aotearoa* is pronounced Ah-aw-tay-ah-raw-ah. The word *Maori,* correctly pronounced, is Mah-aw-ree but Europeans, probably because it is easier, usually say *Mow-ry* to rhyme with *Dowry.*

Over many centuries the Polynesians were probably the greatest pioneer navigators in history—even greater than the Norse-

men, the Greeks, and the Arabs. There is one theory that they entered the Pacific Ocean from the west more than two thousand years before Columbus struck out across the Atlantic Ocean. According to a legend, these early explorers, who were the ancestors of the Maoris, originally came from a land far to the west near Uru, possibly Ur in the Euphrates Valley as mentioned in the Bible. They settled in Irihia, which some anthropologists think is an ancient name for India, but were harassed by the aborigines and, after a time, expelled. Thus started the migrants' long careers as voyagers and colonizers, for it was then that they ventured into the vast Pacific Ocean area. They explored the far-scattered islands and settled in such places as Samoa and Tonga, northward in Hawaii, in the center

The routes of the ancient Polynesian explorers, ancestors of the Maoris of today.

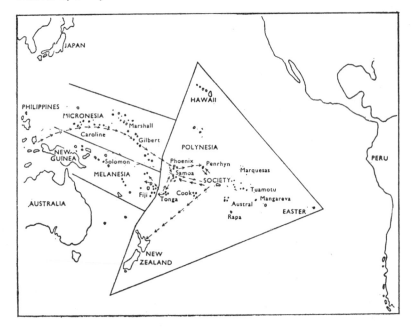

on the Society Islands and in the east on Easter Island. There
is evidence that Polynesians once inhabited the isolated Pitcairn
Islands.

The Polynesian seagoing vessels took various forms, but the
wide-beamed double canoe types were the most commonly used.
The average length for a voyaging canoe was 70 feet. Although
hollowed out by fire and then by hand with crude stone imple-
ments before being finished and rubbed smooth, these vessels
were marvels of symmetrical design. They were strongly constructed and neatly finished with intricate and beautiful carvings covering the bows and tall stern pieces. The paddles, also,
were finely carved. A small hut was built of tightly woven palm
leaves on a platform joining the two vessels amidships. This
was used as a storeroom for articles necessary for a long voyage
and as a shelter during a rough sea. Usually each canoe had a
mast near the bow of one and near the stern of the other. The
triangular sails were fashioned from grasses, closely braided.

When the lookout crew sighted an approaching storm during a long voyage they cried to their Protector, *"Ruhaia te
waka."* Then sea anchors were lowered to steady the vessels
and to lift the bow stormward, mat covers were lashed down,
and two long steer-oars put out. Thus the voyagers calmly rode
out the storm which they called *Hine-moana,* the Ocean Maid's
anger. An unshakable belief in the power of their gods, magic,
and sea monsters endowed the explorers with confidence when
they cut free from land guides and sailed across great unknown
seas, for every vessel, prior to sailing, was blessed by a priestly
expert and placed under a particular god's care.

The early Polynesian explorers possessed considerable knowledge of astronomy; they had names for more than sixty dif-

ferent stars and they knew when to expect certain stars to pass over different islands. This knowledge, combined with the use of crude charts made from stick frames, enabled them to determine the direction of the ocean currents and at what time certain trade winds would blow. The frames were strung with fibers to represent these; small, attached sticks or shells located the known islands. Several specimens of these ingenious charts are preserved in different museums around the world.

New Zealand was the last land to be discovered and settled by descendants of the migrants from Irihia. After Kupe returned to his homeland other voyagers ventured southwestward from Polynesia. Stories and fables were circulated concerning the new land across the ocean. A favorite myth tells how Maui, who figures largely in Maori folklore as a personification of some phase of light representing life, discovered Aotearoa. He took control of his brother's canoe, so the story is told, and sailed it southwest beyond Polynesian waters. When he was hungry he fished, using his grandmother's jaw as a hook and blood from his own nose as bait. Then he pulled up a huge fish, the biggest ever hooked, and named it *Te Ika a Maui,* Maui's Fish. This was the North Island. Maui's canoe was the South Island. Legend and myth, which drew their powers from magic, played a part in everything of importance to the Polynesians. They performed magic, in the form of myths, to secure success in love or in barter. Thus, Maui's fish means the bringing of light and life to Aotearoa.

It is remarkable that an accurate history was possible, for until the early missionaries created one the Maoris had no written language. But each community supported a wise man, or *tohunga,* who memorized not only his tribe's history but the genealogy, or *whakapapa,* of every tribal member. Sometimes this included 1400 names and 450 history songs which the *tohunga* recounted with accompanying gestures from his hands, arms, body, and features. Mnemonic sticks aided the *tohungas'* memories also. These are long, carved and notched sticks which have been in use since ancient times.

So it is told that in about the year 1350 seven vessels arrived in Aotearoa at the same time. This is known as the Great Migration and the names of the vessels were *Te Arawa, Tainui, Matatua, Takitimu, Aotea, Kurahaupo,* and *Tokomaru.* The new arrivals found that Aotearoa was already inhabited by the Moriori, an inferior people about whom little is known. They quickly killed off the Moriori, or drove them away to offshore islands. Occasionally the Moriori were kept as slaves; less frequently there was intermarriage. From time to time other migrants left their homeland and followed the original fleet to Aotearoa. Sometimes they left because of overpopulation, or as refugees from invading enemies, but usually they came to the new land that was rumored to be one of great fertility and spaciousness for the sheer pleasure of exploration. Endowed with enterprise and courage, physical endurance and stamina, the Maoris brought their myths, superstitions, and religions with them and an enduring faith in Io, the Supreme Being who protected them.

The settlement of Aotearoa, by the descendants of the exiles from Irihia, completed what anthropologists call the Great Polynesian Triangle in the Pacific.

Soon the sound of building echoed through the silent forests. Adzes hacked at the fallen trees, for each canoeload of migrants chose the site for its own village, or *pa,* and wasted no time in erecting fortifications. They formed separate communities and henceforth enemies so that the *pas* were constructed with ramparts, stockades, and twenty-foot-deep ditches. These were heavily protected by spikes and each *pa* was enclosed with a series of strong fences. When possible a site was selected where one side faced a river or the sea. Such a location ensured not only ingress and exit but a certainty of fish for food in case of enemy siege.

Among the food supplies brought over miles of ocean from their homeland were *kumaras* (sweet potatoes), taro roots, breadfruit, coconuts, and gourds which were used as containers. The newcomers wasted no time in turning the soil for planting. They used hoes and digging sticks, which were poles pointed at the lower end with an attached step about two feet from the point. Chanting as they worked, the diggers drove these into the ground, using the steps as levers. The vegetables they planted thrived and became staple foods, but the breadfruit and the coconuts were short-lived in Aotearoa's cooler climate. However, starchy foods were found among indigenous plants such as fern roots and raupo (bulrush). The Maoris brought *kiore* rats as pets, for hunting, for food and, while the supply of animals lasted, as skin capes for their chiefs and others of high rank. The Maoris' protein needs were satisfied by the eating of fish, small animals, game birds, and human flesh. Their supply of the latter came, usually, from the vanquished in battle, but on special occasions, such as a chief's wedding, his funeral, or to celebrate the tattooing of his daughter, a slave would be killed and roasted. In most tribes, however, women were forbidden to eat human flesh.

When the days began to shorten and Aotearoa's few deciduous trees dropped their leaves, the Maoris suffered a new experience—they were cold. The bark cloth (*tapa*) worn in their former home was no protection against Aotearoa's winters. A substitute had to be found quickly. The Maoris turned to a fibrous native plant, flax (phormium), which first had to be dressed and spun before being woven or braided. They learned to prepare the long flax leaves by scraping off the green matter until only the fibers remained, splitting them lengthwise; then, by the primitive method of starting with a strong string tied to upright sticks driven into the ground, they braided strips of cloth. This was the work of the women. As time went on they became more adept; the art of dyeing was introduced when fashioning the two garments habitually worn, which were a knee-length kilt and a rectangular cape. Rich reds, yellows, and blacks were deftly used in forming patterns that created garments of great beauty. Sometimes bird feathers were interwoven with the flax, producing a softness and sheen that made the cloth a delight to touch as well as to wear. The women made not only clothing but floor and wall coverings as well, for the wooden houses, or *whares,* that the men built. These *whares,* measuring about 8 by 14 feet, were without windows or chimneys and contained no furniture. However, to make up for their lack of comfort, elaborate carvings and paintings decorated the narrow entrances and the corner posts which rather resembled Indian totem poles.

In time a distinctive type of Maori design evolved which was unlike that of their homeland. Wood carvers were given to using scrolls, spiral designs, and grotesque human figures with protruding tongues. Their distortions of natural forms were not due to lack of skill, for they were superb craftsmen, but to religious

The Maoris are expert wood carvers. (Left) *Interior of a meeting-hall, richly carved.* (Right) *Distinctive facade of a Maori* pataka *or food storehouse.*

scruples against realism in art, which competed with the work of the divine creator. Sometimes they repeated, in their carvings, weird-looking creatures with the heads of birds which probably had a symbolic meaning now forgotten. The only animal to appear frequently was the lizard, which represents Whiro, the symbol of evil and death. Wood carving, with only stone chisels and whalebone mallets as tools, was a tedious task and the carvings on a *whare* of importance meant many years of labor.

But the early Maoris employed this skill, with patience, on many objects. They carved the prows of war canoes, storehouses, ornaments, utensils, and weapons under the watchful eye of Tane, the craftsmen's god.

One ambition every tribe held was to acquire pieces of the hard mineral known to them as *pounamu*. Chunks of this nephrite (greenstone or New Zealand jade) lay in a few river beds on the west coast of the South Island. The Maoris soon learned that this hard stone was a better material for tool blades than any other mineral. Hazardous journeys to where the treasure was located were undertaken under the jealous scrutiny of enemies. The Maoris used heavy stones to break off several large blocks at a time. Upon returning home the pieces were sawn into shape and finally brought to a razor-sharp edge by means of laborious rubbings with sandstone. The Maoris loved *pounamu* for its translucent green beauty in addition to its utilitarian value. They made jewelry; the women cherished their greenstone *tiki* necklaces worn as fertility tokens. This was about the only ornament the women wore; they left personal adornment to the menfolk, who bestowed great attention, with the aid of their wives, to smearing their skins with a mixture of ocher and oil, inserting long greenstone earrings, hanging whales' teeth about their necks, and tying their long hair into a tight knot in which they placed feathers or a comb. In contrast to today's customs, the women customarily wore their hair short in the early days.

To further glorify his appearance every Maori of importance was tattooed, having his face, thighs, and buttocks closely covered with intricate swirls and spirals. For women, tattooing was applied only to the lips and chin except in rare instances. The

Tattoos like these are marks of importance among those Maoris who still follow old traditions. The man's black-and-white feather is also an indication of high rank.

pigment used was made from soot after the burning of a resinous wood or the gum from a kauri pine. The artist first dipped his adze-shaped implement into the pigment, then onto the skin, giving it a sharp tap and causing great pain to the subject of the operation. Even under the apt hands of a skillful craftsman several months were necessary for the completion of such a work of art.

Strong class distinctions existed in Maori *pas* which, in time, increased their numbers into the thousands. The leaders, the Rangatiras, with their fully tattooed faces, were persons of great dignity and importance. Although monogamy was the general practice they alone, under exceptional circumstances, exercised their privilege in taking a second wife. For instance, if a Rangatira's wife proved to be barren or produced only girls, he felt justified in introducing a second wife into his household. Then to insure that future disputes would be kept within the family, the most satisfactory choice was his sister-in-law.

Although schools were conducted exclusively for young Rangatiras, where they were taught the duties pertaining to leadership as well as traditional history, education was the responsibility of grandparents. The able-bodied parents were then free to perform work requiring physical energy.

In place of a code of civil law, the real ruling influence in tribal life was the system of *tapu*, a series of prohibitions with far-reaching powers that entered into every phase of native life. The individual who disregarded the rules of *tapu* was punished, not by his fellow tribesmen, but by the gods themselves, who withdrew their support. Unless he quickly sought the aid of a *tohunga*, or priestly expert, and persuaded him to perform a ceremony lifting the *tapu*, an offender worried himself to death. Certain areas and conditions were regarded as *tapu*. For instance, a person trespassing in a graveyard became *tapu*, or untouchable, and the one attending to the ceremony of burial went through a water-cleansing ordeal both before and after the ceremony. Anything touched by blood was *tapu*, therefore tattooing was conducted in the open rather than subject a house to the inconvenience of becoming *tapu*. In childbirth a woman was banished to a "nest house" where she stayed until after the appropriate ceremony performed by a *tohunga*. Then the "nest house" was burned. During the planting and tending of a *kumara* crop care was taken to preserve the life principle of the plants, otherwise serious consequences could be expected. Workers in the fields sang special songs to immunize themselves as they dug. Later ceremonies were conducted to free the workers from *tapu*. If a worker disregarded this rule everything he touched became *tapu* also.

Laws governing the early Maoris were stringent but just the same they found many occupations and entertainments to bring them happiness in their close-knit communities. Family life was strong and a love for children reached adulation heights. If a child lost his parents he was gathered, lovingly, into an adopted mother's arms.

The Maoris became expert fishermen and bird snarers. From rivers and streams they took crayfish, smaller fish species, and mussels; they built eel weirs across the rivers. The nets used for sea fishing sometimes measured 1000 yards and required 500 people to haul them. One particular net, measured by Europeans many years later, stretched 2090 yards in length. In some areas, when a large catch was taken from the net, the *tohunga* would pluck a hair from his own head, then place it in the mouth of a selected fish. He would face east, holding the fish at arm's length as he chanted. When a new net was hauled a rigid form of *tapu* reigned over the beaches and severe punishment was inflicted on any intruder. Sometimes the fish were returned to the sea except for a few used for ceremonial purposes.

The Maoris devised several varieties of snares and traps for catching small birds, but spears measuring 18 to 30 feet were used for capturing pigeons, considered a great delicacy. Hunters waited on platforms built high in the treetops in places where a flock was likely to pass. A hunter, returning to the *pa* with his string of birds swinging from his spear, would be heard singing, or chanting, as he approached through the woods.

Any excuse served to compose a new song—the loss of an eel pot or the grief of a man afflicted with a skin disease. Many years after the Maoris came to Aotearoa they acquired pigs. One lament was over the death of the first pig a certain village had owned. Although their scale was limited, the Maoris had very fine tonal and rhythmic sense; songs were composed with as many as four parts when even the smallest children were included. *Poi* canoe songs were filled with melody and were also a delight to watch. The singing was accompanied by gentle undulations and swaying of their bodies by the women who sat on the ground, one behind the other, in long lines. As they swayed they flipped *pois*—little balls made of dried raupo leaves filled with fluff—against their forearms and shoulders. These are the words of one *poi* song:

> Pi-Ka-Tu, now up and down glide our canoe,
> Onward to Wa-i-a-ri-ki. See, see how the waves part
> From her prow. Sing I-to-ma-u-na-WA.

Some dance, or *haka,* steps were delivered with tremendous energy; the war haka was such a one. The men roared as they stamped their feet, quivered their fingers, distorted their features, rolled their eyes, and stuck out their tongues. They were careful to keep in unison, for it boded ill for the coming battle if even one performer sang out of tune or time. It must have been a terrifying sight when hundreds of warriors shouted the war *haka* prior to going to war. Musical instruments were limited to handsome shell trumpets, long wooden trumpets, magnificently carved bull-roarers, nose flutes, and a drum, or gong. Somehow the Maoris never got around to inventing any stringed instruments.

Fascinating games were invented, many of them similar to those played by European children. The Maoris used dried raupo leaves for building tremendous kites, or *manus,* sometimes shaped like birds. On contest days Aotearoa's blue skies were dotted with flying kites; their tail feathers fluttered behind them as they skimmed across the sky. The girls played *koruru,* a form of jacks, with quickness and precision. Their fingers were made supple by being pressed back so that with practice they were able to catch the jacks on the backs of their hands as well. And at cat's cradle they had no equal. They made elaborate and intricate designs where several players took part, using toes and teeth to make patterns which had names and which illustrated certain activities pertaining to mythical figures from the past. The boys wrestled (to rules), they walked on stilts and water-jumped on poles. Boys spun both whip tops and humming tops. One favorite pastime was giant stride around the *moari,* a tall pole with long attached ropes, rather like a maypole. After getting up enough momentum a player could sweep over the ground with twelve-foot strides. If the *moari* stood by the seashore it was fun to swing out, drop the rope, and plunge into the water, for at swimming, with a side stroke, Maori children became experts at a very early age. Even the youngest was fearless in water; to be included in canoe or fishing expeditions was a special treat.

One game Maori boys took more seriously than any other was the game of war. They received rigid training in the use of two-handed weapons and in the art of avoiding enemy blows and thrusts. They learned to be nimble in first thrusting with the pointed end, then quickly reversing the swordlike club and delivering a heavy blow with the thick end.

The favorite weapon of fighting men was the *mere,* from 12 to 20 inches in length, made from bone or stone or the prized *pounamu.* A blow from a greenstone *mere* could split a man's skull. The Maoris, although altruistic in their own communities, were ruthless in war, a pastime in which they were constantly indulging. Being sensitive to supposed slights and ridicule from outsiders, they were quick to seek vengeance. When about to hit the war trail warriors (and some women also) underwent a form of baptism which brought them under a special *tapu* of the war god. Fighting was savage and, unless they were incapacitated, to the death, for they bore their minor injuries with equanimity. The first individual killed in battle was termed the "first fish" and honor came to the warrior who achieved this feat. When an enemy chief was killed and eaten, he was considered to have been reduced to the level of common food, and this stigma passed to succeeding generations.

A greater stigma was attached to being captured in battle and having one's life spared for enslavement. Sometimes the victor needed additional labor in his *pa,* but often it was for the personal satisfaction of reducing one of high rank to a degrading position, for even if he escaped, a Maori lost status within his own tribe if once he had been a slave. A slave presented a sad spectacle indeed, for he became permanently separated from his own beloved tribe. No more would he exchange the *hongi,* the nose-pressing symbol of friendship and trust among the Maoris. In despair a slave would beat his head and cry, "Bring me a handful of earth from my home that I may cry over it." Yet a slave, though never becoming a full member, could marry into an enemy's tribe and his children were accepted as members. By constant reminders, however, he knew what fate awaited him for certain misdemeanors in behavior—it was that of the cook oven.

Thus the years rolled by in Aotearoa. Only the first generation of migrants was homesick for the coconuts and breadfruit that failed to thrive, the waving tropical palms and the warm breezes of former days. Succeeding generations became adapted to the new land; it was their home—a healthy one, for no endemic or epidemic diseases existed in pre-European days. But the Maoris never relinquished the belief that when they died their souls leapt from Aotearoa's most northern point, Cape Reinga, to find permanent resting places in their original homeland.

It was three hundred years after the Great Migration that an unfamiliar menace threatened the Maoris. Two strange ships, sailing before a strong wind, came gliding into the strait that separated Maui's fish from Maui's canoe. Perhaps a premonition of disastrous times ahead brought the Ngati-Apa tribesmen bounding down to the foreshore to attack, with more than their usual fury, these unwanted, palefaced intruders. At about that same time, on the other side of the world, an Iroquois Indian was declaring, "The greatest source of all our grievances is that the white men are among us." As it was for the Indians, it was calamitous indeed, for a long time, when Pakehas came to disturb Aotearoa's Maoris in their established way of life.

5

/\/\/\/\/\

Then Came
Sailing Ships

THE WATCHMAN on the mast of the flagship *Heemskerck* must have given an exultant shout of "Land ahoy!" when he sighted the great white ramparts of the Southern Alps rising above the green forests. It was during the morning of December 13, 1642, that the two ships, the *Heemskerck* and the *Zeehaen,* approached the land that sprawled undiscovered by Europeans. They were under the command of Abel Janszoon Tasman, a Hollander and already a noted explorer among Asian islands. Tasman had been chosen by Java's new governor, Antony van Diemen, to seek the legendary great southern continent—"the remaining unknown part of the terrestrial globe." Tasman struck out southwestward from Java across the Indian Ocean until he reached latitude 40° south where the cold but steady westerly winds drove the two ships eastward, far below the long coast line of Australia. Somehow Tasman missed seeing that vast continent which almost equals the United States in area. However, he discovered the island of Tasmania, a green oasis lying to the south. He named the island Van Diemen's Land, in honor of the man who had commissioned him to make this perilous voyage, before he sailed on eastward to discover New Zealand.

Tasman's pilot, Visscher, set a course for the still waters at the entrance to a strait, while Tasman scanned the thin line of coast which he later reported as being some hundreds of miles long, the edge of "a large land, uplifted high." The two ships came to rest in a wide sheltered bay, the sails were furled, the anchors dropped, and Tasman prepared to land. The landing boats, loaded with men agog with excitement and anticipation, were oared toward the gold-sanded beach. Suddenly, from behind one low headland, a fleet of canoes came speeding toward them. Maori warriors, armed to the hilt with clubs and spears, fell upon the surprised newcomers with savage ferocity. In the bloody clash that followed four sailors were killed, the boats were driven back, and Tasman was forced to give up attempts at landing. Volleys were fired from the *Heemskerck* and the *Zeehaen* at the wrathful Maoris who were in hot pursuit.

Tasman, saddened by the loss of his men, named the place Murderers Bay, then he weighed anchor and sailed off northward back to Java by way of Fiji and the north coast of New Guinea. Later, Murderers Bay was renamed Golden Bay. On Tasman's map the new country is called Statenlandt, but geographers soon changed the name to Nieuw Zeeland after a province in Holland. The Maoris watched until the European ships, with sails billowing like large white birds, dropped below the

ENGRAVING FROM FRANCOIS VALENTYN'S JOURNAL, 1726
Tasman's clash with Maori warriors in "Murderer's Bay."

horizon, then they resumed their communal existence, their fighting, and their primitive methods of wresting sustenance from the land and from the sea. New Zealand's coast line remained an uncharted mystery; it was left alone for another hundred and twenty-seven years.

For many years men of science had discussed the possibility

Captain James Cook, R.N., in about 1776.

of New Zealand's being part of a mass of dry land reaching up from antarctic regions, a Great South Land that surely existed in order to balance the earth. At last an opportunity came for further exploration; an expedition was organized that would serve a double purpose. The year was 1768 and the planet Venus was expected to pass between earth and the sun. As the Polynesian island of Tahiti was the best vantage point for observation the bark *Endeavour* was commandeered to convey a group of scientists out to the Pacific. Lieutenant James Cook, a fearless man and, like the Polynesians, a great navigator, was placed in command by the British Admiralty. They sailed out around Cape Horn, then north across the equator to Tahiti in the Northern Hemisphere.

The astronomical expedition having completed its mission successfully, Cook turned his attention to the second assignment, that of finding the Great South Land. With eagerness he sailed southwestward and, on October 8, 1769, he rediscovered New Zealand. The surgeon's boy, Nicholas Young, was the first to sight a point of land on the east coast. This point is still called Young Nick's Head. The *Endeavour* moved into the adjacent bay but, when a boat party attempted to land, Maoris attacked. In the ensuing scuffle one Maori was shot, much to Cook's regret, before the party could withdraw. However, Cook persisted; next day he again tried to land and to befriend the natives. He took a Tahitian cabin boy, Tupia, along to act as interpreter but, though Tupia's language was understood, it was impossible to quiet the Maoris. Again they attacked ferociously and again one Maori was shot. Cook succeeded in capturing three native boys whom he took aboard ship, thinking that with a display of kindness the Maoris would be convinced of his good intentions; the boys were surprised and pacified by the good treatment they received, but when placed on land again the hundreds of Maoris lining the shore still presented a united, belligerent front. Cook, in disgust, named the place Poverty Bay—a real misnomer, for that region is one of New Zealand's richest farming areas. He sailed south along the coast until the *Endeavour* came to another tribe's territory. Here Lieutenant Cook met with success in befriending the natives to such an extent that a few of them, in unabashed curiosity, consented to staying aboard ship overnight.

Cook reversed his course at a point he named Turnagain; he sailed back north past Poverty Bay until he found a tribe so friendly that he and his party were escorted through their *pa,* the hosts explaining the complex code of living and law as the guests examined the houses and storerooms and admired the symbolic carvings. After bartering with these friendly people for food, Cook named the place Mercury Bay. Then he raised the British flag and took possession of New Zealand for England. Cook continued north, swinging around North Cape, then down the west coast to the bay where Tasman had met with disaster. Cook thoroughly explored the strait that he named for himself. While there he took possession of the South Island, also, for England. Upon reaching Cape Turnagain, Cook brought the *Endeavour* about, being certain that this was an island. He then circled New Zealand's South Island and, upon returning to Cook Strait, left New Zealand behind him to sail across the stormy Tasman Sea to discover Australia.

Lieutenant Cook, who later was promoted to a captain's rank, kept complete records of his findings. He was quick to see and to note the new land's potentialities; he made a detailed map, with amazingly few errors, which subsequent explorers found invaluable. Perhaps as great a contribution as his discoveries, however, were the friendly relations he established, on the whole, with the Maoris. Cook thought, wrongly, that the Maoris' cannibal habits came from a need for animal foods; he endeared himself to several tribes with presents of pigs, sheep, and goats as well as chickens, potatoes, cabbages, and other vegetables. A mysterious weed killed the sheep and the goats, but the pigs and chickens thrived and multiplied.

Unknown to either, another European was sailing New Zealand waters at the same time that Cook was making his careful survey. A French navigator, Jean-François de Surville, in the ship *St. Jean Baptiste,* came down from the Solomon Islands.

He anchored in a bay that he named Lauriston, but Lieutenant Cook, eight days previously, had pulled in there and named it Doubtless Bay. Thanks to Cook, De Surville found the Maoris friendly. Unfortunately, because he suspected that some of them had stolen a boat, he punished them by burning their village and kidnaping their chief. De Surville sailed away never to return, for he died, shortly afterward, in Peru. But two years later another Frenchman, Marion du Fresne, crossed the Tasman Sea from Tasmania. He dropped anchor in the Bay of Islands where the natives appeared friendly. Suddenly, after a month's stay there, Du Fresne and twenty-six companions were set upon, killed, then eaten. The reasons for this ghastly assault are vague; it is thought by some historians that Du Fresne violated one particularly strict *tapu* by using sacred images as firewood. Maori law demanded that they must die, but Du Fresne's second in command saw the Maoris only as brutal savages. He destroyed their possessions and hunted out and shot down every warrior he could find. Terrible repercussions resulted from these incidents, which remained in Maori memory for many years. Even after England had established a colony in New Zealand chiefs appealed for protection against the "tribe of Marion."

New Zealand's fascinations drew Captain Cook to her shores three times. On the second visit he and his crew rested for a time by Dusky Sound in Fiordland. He found pleasure there in hunting wild fowl and in fishing. When not searching for succulent mussels Cook and his men captured seals, the flesh of which they ate, using the oil for lamps and the skins for rigging. To him it was an idyllic interlude.

The rich discoveries in the Pacific area during the eighteenth century turned Europe's close attention in that direction. It was conjectured that a shorter route from Europe must exist than the ones around the Cape of Good Hope or Cape Horn. Perhaps a passage by sea could be found up north in the arctic region. An expedition was organized in 1776 and Captain Cook was the man chosen to lead it by way of the Indian and Pacific oceans. It turned out to be Cook's last voyage of exploration.

For the third time Captain Cook sailed through Cook Strait, then for the first time north across the equator and into the Northern Hemisphere. In 1778 he discovered the Hawaiian Islands (which he named the Sandwich Islands) before the two sloops of war, *Resolution* and *Discovery,* continued northward. They skirted the shores of Oregon, then continued along the coast, through the Bering Strait, and into the Arctic Ocean. It was a heroic effort but, for sailing ships, an impossibility to penetrate the ice-blocked passage. As the season closed Captain Cook turned about and sailed due south. For fifty-one days Cook, in the *Resolution,* sailed through waters surrounding Maui and Hawaii islands, seeking safe anchorage. At last the two sloops came to rest in Kealakekua Bay.

Captain Cook's entry in his journal for that day, January 17, 1779, includes, "The ships . . . were surrounded by a multitude of canoes. I had nowhere, in the course of my voyages, seen so numerous a body of people assembled at one place. For beside those in the canoes, all the shore was covered with spectators, and many hundreds were swimming round the ship like shoals of fish. . . ." He was soon to learn the reason for this demonstration. The Hawaiian Polynesians had recognized Captain Cook as their god, Orono, who had prophesied his return in a great ship bearing a forest of trees. Cook was escorted ashore with elaborate ceremony, then he was decked in sacred red cloth before being fed with *kava* and pork, previously chewed, as a symbol. During three days of celebration gifts of fruit, flowers, meats, and costly garments were bestowed upon him. The adulation reached such heights that Cook became alarmed. He grew easier when the ships, having been refitted by February 4, spread their white sails and glided from the bay.

But that night, and in the days to follow, terrible storms swept the ocean, the white sails were split, the *Resolution's* foremast was sprung, the winds drove them back to Kealakekua Bay— not in triumph but as defeated gods. On February 11, Kealakekua Bay was a port of distress for the *Resolution* and the *Discovery*. Captain Cook was no longer Orono but a distraught ship commander. And adulation turned to mistrust and suspicion among his Polynesian friends. Mounting friction between Cook's crew and the natives became open hostility.

When Captain Cook sought to avenge the theft of one landing boat on February 14, the Hawaiians attacked with stones and pikes and, under the barrage, four marines were killed and several wounded. In their defense the marines retaliated with gunfire. Cook's orders to desist were ineffective as the mob of angry natives pressed closer. He reached the edge of the beach, then turned to shout an order for his boats to stop firing and to come in, but a god never turns his back. This was the signal for the Hawaiians to strike. With a heavy stone on his head and a stab wound in his back, Captain Cook fell dead.

It was ironic that the man who had extended understanding and sympathy, who had worked to establish improved relations between European and Polynesian, should meet with the same fate as Du Fresne and his companions. Today a monument stands by the shore of Kealakekua Bay to the memory of Captain Cook, who held his own so valiantly during all the voyages of discovery he made throughout the blue Pacific Ocean.

6

/\\.\\.\\.\\.\\.\\

Timber Getters, Whalers, and Missionaries

DUSKY SOUND, the beautiful spot in Fiordland where Captain Cook sojourned for a while, became the location for the first European house. In 1792 the sealing vessel *Britannia* left men in Dusky Sound for ten months. The sealers built a house; later, when they became fearful that they had been forgotten, they built a seventy-ton schooner as a possible means of escape. In the interval these first recorded sealers killed and skinned over 4000 seals, which later fetched a good price in Sydney, Australia.

New Zealand's fame as a rich source for seals, whales, and timber, combined with Cook's glowing accounts of the new country, enticed sailing ships by the hundreds early in the nineteenth century. Ships came, not only from Britain, but from all corners of the earth, including Maine and other eastern states of North America. The slaughter of seals was so systematically conducted that before long the industry petered out. For the same reason, after a few years, many shore whaling stations that had been set up to catch the baleen whales, come to New Zealand to breed, had to be abandoned.

New Zealand's forests grew right to the water's edge. The tall straight kauri pines were carried away in timber ships as fast as they could be sawn down. They made excellent masts and spars for ships as well as building boards and paving blocks for European streets. The largest timber tree ever felled came from a New Zealand forest. With a girth of 72 feet and, approximately, a 24-foot diameter, its trunk measured 80 feet to the first branch. The forests and the slow-growing kauri pines

A kauri pine tree. It took nearly 300 years for this giant to reach its present size, dwarfing a man seen hugging a trailing rata vine.

were almost devastated before the traffic in timber was stopped.

The easy wealth of the early days of New Zealand brought adventurers, fugitives from justice, and deserters from the penal colonies in Australia. It was inevitable that these undesirable characters should clash with the Maoris, whose complex social system they failed to respect even when capable of comprehending it. With no high authority to enforce law and order, contacts between Europeans and Maoris ended in bloodshed and dreadful deeds more often than otherwise. Some early visitors turned native and married Maori women—they became Pakeha-Maoris. A few good men, who sincerely adopted the Maori way of life, exerted a favorable influence on both the Maoris and the Pakehas; it was through such men that many puzzling native customs were made understandable. But, on the whole, the early influences were vicious and lawless.

When trading posts were established Europeans exchanged cloth, working tools, muskets, and gunpowder for food and indigenous flax, which proved strong material for roping. Unfortunately it took only a short time for Maori warriors to learn to handle muskets and what effective weapons they made against their enemies. Many tribes accelerated their activities in the preparation of flax, their best medium of exchange, in order to acquire more and more muskets and gunpowder. As a result, tribal warfare blazed throughout New Zealand's North Island in addition to repeated incidents against the Pakehas who broke the sacred laws of *tapu* again and again.

Such incidents culminated in the horrible *Boyd* massacre in 1809. The *Boyd,* a trading ship from Sydney, had dropped anchor in Whangaroa Harbor to take on a load of kauri spars. One crew member was a Maori chief and it was within sight of his own home, his *pa,* that the *Boyd* had anchored. For an unexplained misbehavior, the *Boyd's* skipper flogged the chief on his back and on his head, thus committing the most atrocious violation of all, for a chief's back, and particularly his head, are at all times sacred and *tapu.* The insulted and infuriated tribesmen slaughtered all but four persons of forty aboard the *Boyd,* then, some records say, they ate them. Finally they set the ship afire. The four who were spared, a woman and three children, were saved by a neighboring chief. When whalers from the Bay of Islands rescued the survivors they also, in reprisal, burned two villages, one of which belonged to the chief who had come to the rescue. Later, Whangaroa tribesmen killed the sympathetic chief for his part in the affair. The *Boyd* massacre was the worst Pakeha incident in the early days. Details of the massacre's horrors reached the ears of the Reverend Samuel Marsden in Sydney; he resolved to introduce Christianity into that heathen land.

The Reverend Mr. Marsden, a Church of England chaplain and a kindly man, had held a keen interest in the intelligent, courteous Maoris ever since he had traveled on the same ship from England with a young warrior, nephew of Hongi, chief of the Bay of Islands tribe. The clergyman was already arranging to send missionaries to New Zealand when the news came of the ghastly *Boyd* massacre. Thereupon the governor in Sydney induced Marsden to abandon the project. The governor, however, issued an order making the owner of every ship that traded with New Zealand responsible for the behavior of his crew. Five thousand dollars was the fine for any disobedience of this order. Five years later Marsden succeeded in winning the governor's consent to carry the Christian faith to the Maoris of New Zealand. During the year 1814 he sailed from Sydney for the Bay of Islands district. Two other missionaries, a resident magistrate, and workmen accompanied him, together with livestock, for his purpose was to establish a permanent settlement under the protection of his shipboard friend's uncle, Chief Hongi. Thus, on Christmas Day, 1814, beneath the waving British flag, the first Christian service was held before a vast congregation assembled to hear the doctrines of love and peace.

The Reverend Mr. Marsden's duties recalled him to Sydney but the two remaining missionaries, with others who came later, conscientiously threw themselves into the task of converting the Maoris while educating them by means of the written word. Missionaries translated the Bible and other books into the Maori language; they trained them in singing when it was found that the Maoris' clear, high voices were adaptable to the diatonic scale; they discouraged the Maori habits of keeping slaves, cannibalism, and other barbarous practices. It was the missionaries who introduced garden flowers, sheep, and cows to New Zealand. Many were great travelers, brave men who ventured into hostile territory; some gave their lives.

Sometimes the missionaries' well-intentioned efforts were hampered by the Maoris' ambitions for conquest; their natural love of fighting became exaggerated with the availability of muskets and gunpowder supplied by despicable Pakehas who settled among them. For a time chivalry and the rules of war, as practiced in the early days, gave way to tyranny. Smaller tribes, unable to pay the price for arms, fell before the onslaught of a few mighty and powerful chiefs; New Zealand's North Island was held in a constant state of terror. Even Chief Hongi, protector of the missions, finally burst the bonds of his promise to keep the peace. He stormed through the island dispersing and destroying tribe after tribe. When Hongi attacked the pioneer Arawa tribe who guarded the Maoris' most sacred relics, a united army marched against the tyrant. But until the day he died Hongi proved unconquerable.

One story has been preserved as an example of how, despite conflicting beliefs, some Maori warriors practiced the new doctrines brought by the missionaries. The Maori King Tawhiao's early training had been in the pagan religion—the power of legendary lore—but he was a thoughtful man who appreciated the principles of Christianity. Some years later, when war had broken out between the Maoris and British soldiers, Tawhiao, with his 2000 followers, were stationed in their well-fortified *pa* with the attacking British soldiers encamped at some distance. One day a flotilla, comprising several large canoes, came down the river from Tawhiao's *pa*. The leading canoe bore a white flag and, when stopped, the Maori warrior in charge explained that Tawhiao, upon hearing that the British garrison suffered from a shortage of provisions, had obeyed the Bible injunction, "If thine enemy hunger, give him meat; if he thirst, give him drink." The canoes contained several tons of potatoes, other vegetables, and milking goats as a present to his enemies from Tawhiao.

The mission people in London had declared themselves the protectors of the Maoris; they opposed European colonization, saying it would bring corruption to Maori health and morals. But many Maoris had already succumbed to European diseases such as measles, to which they had no resistance. Their numbers had shrunk deplorably since Captain Cook's coming. Some

Maoris suffered no less from the confusion wrought by the loss of their old pagan beliefs and the new Christian faith which they found, upon adoption, was not always practiced by the Pakehas they encountered as it was preached by the missionaries.

One particularly bloody episode, which drew the South Island into the conflict and involved an English sea captain, was but one factor of three that helped to bring matters to a head, forcing Britain into formal annexation. By this time even the Reverend Mr. Marsden was urging the government to establish some sort of authority. The British government, in 1839, was reluctant to start a new colony; it had enough troubles with its colonies already, politically in Canada, racially in South Africa. But in addition to the scandalous strife within New Zealand, French ships prowled around her coast. It was rumored that a French sea captain had acquired land on the South Island's east coast. France was preparing to establish a colony. The third factor, within England itself, was a formation of the New Zealand Company by Edward Gibbon Wakefield, an ambitious propagandist. Having been denied government support for his scheme of settlement, he and his company acted quietly and without authority. In the British Isles they sold subdivided New Zealand land to prospective settlers before it was purchased from the Maoris. When the government became aware of the advanced state of the enterprise and the fact that the company had already completed the outfitting of several vessels for the conveyance of its customers, it at last was stirred into action. Lieutenant Governor Hobson, chosen as England's representative, hurriedly prepared for the journey, then sailed away for New Zealand with emergency orders to negotiate with the Maori chiefs. What land he could buy from them was to become part of the colony of New South Wales, Australia. No other land sales were to be recognized until after a full investigation by the governor. Thus, three separate expeditions were speeding toward the opposite side of the world during the year 1839.

Colonel Wakefield, a brother of the original promoter of the New Zealand Company who had been placed in charge of a preliminary expedition to buy land, steered for Cook Strait. A French company, commissioned by its government to acquire as much territory as possible, headed for Akaroa in the South Island. Governor Hobson's sights were set on the oldest settlement in the Bay of Islands. Colonel Wakefield won the race. His ship touched New Zealand soil on August 16. His subsequent hurried negotiations with Maori chiefs started a series of land disputes with far-reaching, unhappy, and prolonged effects on the settlement's future.

7

Of Schemes and Acts

THE WAKEFIELD SCHEME, as organized in London by the New Zealand Company, was at first a well-planned attempt to establish the best type of British middle-class settler in New Zealand. But while selling the promise of a "Better Britain" in the "Paradise of the Pacific" to interested would-be migrants with a desire to improve their circumstances the company, in time, turned to exploiting them. New Zealand land, to the value of $500,000 as yet unacquired by the company, was sold prior to the dispatching of more than one thousand hopeful persons across the stormy, unknown seas.

Colonel Wakefield, in the advance ship *Tory,* acted quickly when he landed in Port Nicholson, the future site of Wellington, for news reached him that missionaries were headed in his direction to stop the enterprise. Although he had been carefully instructed to make sure that each land transaction was understood by the Maoris, he made no attempt to heed these instructions. In less than three months he had purchased territory, equal in area to Ireland, which he paid for in goods amounting to only $45,000. Wakefield failed to consult chiefs of all the tribes. A coast line extending for fifty miles near Wellington was acquired from but three chiefs who put their marks on the document he presented. Unaware that they were signing away their lands and those of other tribes as well, the chiefs showed more interest in the division of the glittering piles of scissors, cloth, beads, and other trinkets Wakefield spread before them. Moreover, by Maori law, land belonged to the tribe, never to the individual; it could only be disposed of by a solemn act involving the whole tribe—unless, of course, they lost it to invaders.

Lieutenant Governor Hobson was fully cognizant of the illegal proceedings in the south. Soon after his arrival in the Bay of Islands during January 1840, he called on Mr. James Busby, the official British Resident, in Waitangi. Together they drew up a paper as a protection for the Maoris, then as many chiefs as he could summon listened to a translated reading of its terms. The treaty contained three clauses. The first clause gave Queen Victoria "all the rights and powers of sovereignty held by the chiefs," the second clause guaranteed "full and undisturbed possession of their lands"—but should they wish to sell at any time it must first be offered to the government—and the third clause gave "all the rights and privileges of British subjects" to the Maoris. For two days and nights the Maori chiefs discussed and debated the document's every angle. Then, on Feb-

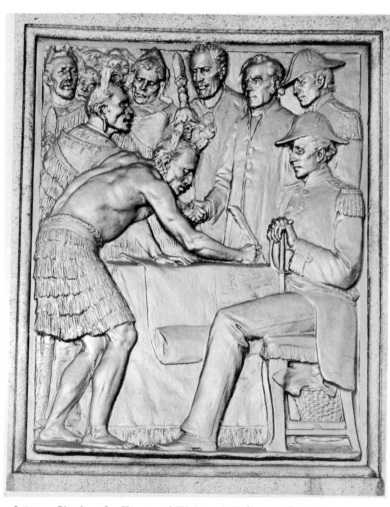

Signing the Treaty of Waitangi, February 6, 1840.
Taken from the bronze plaque on the statue of
Queen Victoria in Wellington. (Left) *Signatures*
to the Treaty of Waitangi.

ruary 6, 1840, about forty leading chiefs signed what came to
be called the Treaty of Waitangi. With its signing New Zealand
became a Crown Colony with the Maoris living under the protection of the governor. Later the treaty was signed by many
more chiefs throughout New Zealand who appreciated the protection it provided. And although in later years Maoris and
Pakehas waged war as a result of land disputes when clauses
within the treaty were threatened, the Treaty of Waitangi retained the respect of everyone as the charter of the Maoris.

Hobson had sent the Treaty of Waitangi through the South
Island also, for signatures; by virture of the treaty and Captain
Cook's discovery, he formally annexed that land for Britain.
This action forestalled the establishment of a French settlement
in Akaroa, their ship having been delayed en route until August
1840. By the time the French arrived a British warship was
anchored off Akaroa's shores. However, the French settlers were
allowed to occupy the land their company had bought and to
live there, in peace, for many years.

Eventually Governor Hobson moved his headquarters from
the Bay of Islands to Auckland. Colonel Wakefield clung to
Wellington. He jeered at the missionaries who were friends of
the governor and blamed every disputed land claim on government, for the Treaty of Waitangi endangered Wakefield's
enterprise. The treaty's clause forbidding the Maori chiefs to
sell supposedly put a stop to his fraudulent transactions, but
when newly arrived immigrants clamored for the land they had
bought and Governor Hobson investigated the claims in 1842,
he found that more than half of New Zealand had been dis-
posed of, on paper, during the past two years. Many claims
overlapped, some were non-existent. Instances occurred repeat-

edly where the new settlers were driven off by the lawful Maori owners. Yet the Maoris exercised tremendous restraint—for a time. Where they found land marked out after survey, they quietly removed the pegs during the night. When huts were built on Maori land they destroyed them, but they carefully preserved the huts' contents. Where a prospecting newcomer found coal on his property and dug it out, after dark the Maoris replaced the coal in the pits.

Some of the disillusioned pioneer colonists, forced to accommodate themselves to this alien land or perish, found solace in writing. A spate of verse flowed from the pens of discouraged, lonely Britons during the mid-nineteenth century. One disenchanted colonist, Dr. Rouse, wrote:

But I have located here no alternative, I fear,
But to make the best of thee, only longing to be free;
Patiently to bear thy clime and anticipate the time
When, my transportation o'er, I shall seek some genial shore,
Never to return to thee, Eden of the Southern Sea.

Harassed by the turbulence created by Wakefield's claimants and the increasing suspicions of some Maori chiefs that the treaty had let them down, Governor Hobson died at his post, a dispirited man, in September 1842. His colony was in heavy debt, his people were dissatisfied and in despair, but Hobson's virtue showed in the justice he meted out to both Maori and Pakeha. As one chief wrote to Queen Victoria, "Let the new governor be a good man, as the governor who has just died."

Conditions had about reached boiling point when an old and bloodthirsty warrior, Te Rauparaha of the Ngati-Toa tribe, plunged into the fray with fervor. He was one who, having signed

Colonel Wakefield's original paper, later learned his mistake. The chief's career was memorable for the march he led his people from the battle-ridden lands terrorized by Hongi. After a hazardous journey they had settled on the shores of Cook Strait with headquarters on Kapiti, a small offshore island. It was convenient for making mainland raids on enemy tribes and for trading with passing ships for muskets and gunpowder—articles Te Rauparaha valued. In 1843, Wakefield's company was momentarily embarrassed by insufficient land for division among a newly arrived group of settlers who had bought blocks on Cook Strait. Wakefield confiscated some of Te Rauparaha's land by the Wairau River in the South Island, for the chief's territory extended across Cook Strait. Te Rauparaha acted. With his tattooed face set grimly and his cape held tightly around him, he grasped his musket and led a flotilla of canoes across the strait. He burned the surveyors' huts and ripped out their markers. With other warrior chiefs and his son-in-law, he camped on the spot. Captain Wakefield (a third Wakefield brother) hurried to the site with a police force; they tried to arrest the chief. "This is our land," Te Rauparaha cried, "Do we go to Europe and steal your land?" Wakefield ignored the exclamations; with his police force, he moved in for an arrest. One policeman fired and a Maori woman, Te Rauparaha's daughter, was shot. Maori restraint gave way at last. "They have begun it," shouted the chiefs, "welcome darkness and death!" A rush of Maoris swept the Englishmen up and over the hill, killing nineteen of them in the struggle, including Captain Wakefield. Te Rauparaha, filled with an ungovernable rage, snatched the handcuffs intended to manacle him and streaked back to the North Island. He called to his fellow tribesmen to join him in clearing all

Pakehas from the land. A missionary and one young Maori chief alone, by tactful handling, prevented the immediate destruction of Wellington. About 30,000 settlers lived, by this time, in various communities; the rumblings of discontent among the Maoris and ominous forebodings of more outbreaks caused a chill of uneasiness to move through more than a few of them.

The new governor's handling of the incident did nothing to improve relations between Maori and Pakeha. Governor Fitzroy first scolded the Wakefield people, then he crossed to Kapiti Island and interviewed Te Rauparaha. He told him how wrong it had been to kill in cold blood, but because the Pakehas were the first to transgress he would refrain from seeking vengeance. Te Rauparaha had expected punishment by his old traditions and honorable beliefs. For the Pakehas to seek no vengeance for the death of kinsmen, nor land where their blood was spilled, was a cowardly act to the Maoris. The story was passed from tribe to tribe; Maoris swaggered and took on airs of superiority. One chief even invited the governor to come share a review of his warrior forces only two miles from Auckland.

The Wairau River affair and its consequences frightened shipping traffic from New Zealand's shores; a necessary customs duty, to help fill the empty coffers, cut off trade with whalers. When the Maoris grumbled because of the cessation of trade in flax and whale oil an American Pakeha pointed to the British flag floating above the settlement in the Bay of Islands. "That's what's wrong," he said, so Hone Heke, a son-in-law of Hongi, marched his men into the village, tore down the flag, and burned it while his warriors performed a war *haka* around the flagpole. Governor Fitzroy, upon hearing of the incident, rushed troops to the incendiary scene but neighboring chiefs quickly apologized and Fitzroy's wrath, like the burning flag, simmered down and flickered out.

Then came disturbing news from London where it had been declared, in the House of Commons, that the Treaty of Waitangi was an injudicious mistake, that the Maoris had no right to un-occupied land since New Zealand was bursting with settlers who had no place to settle. This was but a political move against the Tories, but the Maoris saw it as a threat to their precious land rights. Again Hone Heke marched to the settlement and cut down the flag; again a body of troops was sent to set it up and, this time, to stand guard. Fitzroy offered a reward of $500 for Heke's capture; Heke replied with the same offer for Fitzroy's head. Heke stormed the settlement, burned it to the ground and, for a third time, the flag and flagpole as well.

When news of this disloyal demonstration reached other towns and settlements their occupants panicked. Fortifications were set up speedily; guards stood at attention around the clock. One powerful tribe offered, contemptuously, to protect Fitzroy against Hone Heke. Disgraced, Fitzroy was recalled to London. Another man, experienced in the delicate technique of coloniz-ing and in dealings with conniving land companies, replaced him.

8

/\\/\\/\\/\\
⸱⸱⸱⸱⸱⸱⸱⸱

The Maori Wars

CAPTAIN GEORGE GREY was chosen as Governor Fitzroy's successor. A great administrator and a man of grim determination, he was brought to New Zealand from South Australia, another new colony, where he had already had dealings with the Wakefield company.

War had broken out between the colonists and the Maoris when Grey arrived in Auckland in 1845. He wasted no time in announcing his policy. It was first to subdue the Maoris and then befriend them, win their confidence and, at all times, to protect them and their interests. He proclaimed, at every opportunity, the validity of the Treaty of Waitangi and that it was his intention to stand by its terms. Then he gave every Maori chief a choice, to be friend or enemy. There were to be no neutrals.

Within ten days of Governor Grey's arrival he stood beneath the walls of Hone Heke's strongly fortified *pa* in the Bay of Islands where he delivered an ultimatum to the unruly chief. He gave Hone Heke four days to surrender. The chief refused, so Grey brought up his troops—soldiers, seamen, volunteer colonists, and friendly Maoris—and, with shots from his heaviest cannons, broke through a portion of the blockade, but strong resistance barred further penetration. The besieged Maori garrison was delighted. Here was war as it should be played! It reminded them of the old days—savage fighting with no quarter given. It was a game they understood. Then came Sunday. Heke and his fellow warriors left the *pa* by a secret, rear exit in order to hold service and to cook their meals in the open, for they thought the war game, like any other, should not be played on Sunday. But the British entered through the broken wall and seized Heke's *pa* and, although Heke's garrison made gallant efforts to recapture their stronghold, they were eventually driven off. This dubious victory restored British prestige.

The governor hurried to Wellington where Te Rauparaha and the Port Nicholson tribes were making night raids on the settlers. Grey succeeded in capturing the wily old chief, then held him in a kind of honorable captivity aboard the frigate *Calliope* to keep him out of mischief. Te Rauparaha wore a naval officer's uniform aboard ship and, given to lyrical speechmaking, more than once announced, "Let no man think that I abide in grief . . . I abide here as a chief, and my abode is the abode of a chief."

The subduing of Hone Heke and Te Rauparaha with other instances of Grey's power and justice were recognized throughout the land. Peace, for a time, returned to New Zealand. Governor Grey had won the Maoris' respect; in a short time he won their confidence. He turned his attention to learning the Maori language and to studying their traditions and customs so that he might be better able to understand them. He trained older chiefs as magistrates to keep order within the tribes and young chiefs for the police force. Governor Grey built roads uniting the scattered settlements. Where it was necessary to construct a road through unfriendly Maori territory, he used tact. Grey sent a horse and carriage to one protesting chief as a gift for his wife; accompanied by a note, he explained that driving was good for the health. In his campaign for peace, Grey released Te Rauparaka who, still wearing his naval officer's uniform, returned to his home.

To remedy friction with the colonists, however, presented a more difficult task. The discords were always to do with land tenure. When Grey resumed one of Governor Hobson's original rules that no more than 2560 acres should be granted to any one person, large landowners turned against him. But the Wake-fields remained Grey's strongest antagonists. The company had many powerful friends within the Colonial Office in England. In 1847 Governor Grey received a charter and a set of instructions setting up a constitution that excluded the Maoris and many Europeans from a share in their own government. Among other amendments, the charter denied the terms of the Treaty of Waitangi by abolishing Maori rights to land not actually occupied by them. With his new but uncertain peace, Grey saw this proclamation as a critical point in New Zealand's history. He acted boldly by refusing to obey the new charter's demands. Instead he sent petitions with thousands of signatures to the Colonial Office, along with letters from the bishop and the chief justice. Maori chiefs wrote to Wairiki (Queen Victoria), begging for her intervention. The Colonial Office, staggering under the pile of protests, yielded all along the line and the Waitangi Treaty stood.

Governor Grey's victory finished the New Zealand Company and the Wakefield brothers. The company's funds were exhausted and its reputation had chilled the enthusiasm of any new settlers. Moreover, the acts granting an original loan to the company stipulated that the sum must be repaid by 1850. The New Zealand Company was forced to surrender its charter to the Crown. But active government-assisted colonization continued; thriving centers sprang up throughout both the North and the South Islands.

English settlers arriving in Lyttleton in December, 1850. They have disembarked from the four sailing ships in the harbor, and are climbing up the hill toward the fertile plains.

Governor Grey was knighted; he became Sir George Grey. He was given a free hand in drawing up a New Zealand charter which took the form of six Provincial Councils under a central government. Thus, in 1852, after seven years of his capable administration, New Zealand became a self-governing federation. Having brought New Zealand to the point of self-government, Sir George Grey's thoughts turned to his retirement. He had given seventeen years, with but three months' leave, of overseas service to his country. After the first assembling of the Provincial Councils in 1853 he requested a leave of absence. But, having proved his value in setting wrongs to rights, Sir George was persuaded into going to yet another trouble spot, the disorganized colony in South Africa.

After Sir George Grey went away his new-won peace suffered a sharp setback. Friction that developed between the central authorities and the provinces was easily remedied by letting the provinces have their own way, but more ominous was a new national awareness growing among the Maoris, brought about by a realization that they were being slowly disinherited from their beloved land, their home for five centuries. At a great council of chiefs near Lake Taupo in 1854, a resolution was passed to cease selling any land to the Pakehas, including the authorities. A decision was reached, also, to elect one chief to be "King" as a representative of all the Maoris. Rather than an act of rebellion, this movement was intended as a means of raising them to equal standing with white colonists under the new constitution. Potatau, the first elected "King," was a friend of the Pakehas, so the movement, at first, attracted little attention. Only when a few white settlers thought to buy additional land blocks in order to widen their properties did the spark of discontent ignite and blaze into war. The scene was by the Waitara River in the Taranaki District, a neighborhood of small tribes which quarreled constantly among themselves. However, when surveyors came to measure the land, the Maoris united and converged about the scene. Young warriors, eager to resume their favorite war game, found it easy enough to start a conflagration. War broke out, spread to the Waikato Region, flared for a while, and then died down. The white settlers breathed easier; they relaxed and resumed digging out their farms from forests, a task they had tenaciously set themselves to complete. The disappointed young warriors returned to the fortified *pas* they had constructed in Taranaki's deep forests.

Presently there emerged a new form of religion from Taranaki's hinterland, an evil sect constructed from the knowledge gained from Christianity combined with their forefathers' pagan beliefs; it was filled with the dogma of cruelty, mutilation, cannibalism, and other horrors from the past. Adherents to this new, garbled religion came to be called Hau-Haus, for they believed that no bullet would hurt them nor sword pierce them if, when they charged, they shouted "Hau! Hau!" to the angel Gabriel, their god. Hau-Hau missionaries percolated through the North Island, exciting tribes into becoming converts. But many chiefs defied the Hau-Haus; they fought bravely and independently of government to put down the fanatics.

It seemed that governors who possessed Sir George Grey's administrative talents and knowledge of New Zealand's natives were non-existent. In 1861 he was recalled in a hurry to exercise his influence. The Governor faced three major problems— to exterminate, at all costs, the evil Hau-Hau superstition, to render harmless the rebellious element of the "King" movement, and to appease Maori friends within the movement by satisfying their just demands.

At times Sir George was beset with difficulties from all sides. Because of an unsatisfactory handling of the mile-square block of land by the Waitara River, fierce fighting erupted and raged, out of control, throughout the North Island. Repeated acts of bravery and chivalry were evidenced on both sides but the slaughter, over ten turbulent years, counted into the thousands. When land was set aside as army posts and encampments during the war, dissenting tribes within the "King" movement created Te Aukati (the boundary line) as a demonstration of protest. This was a large tract of land extending west from Lake Taupo to the sea and for a distance north and south. The governor readily agreed to the existence of Te Aukati as a dwelling place for rebellious tribes. Henceforth it was to be called the King Country. Loyal Maoris and Pakehas were forbidden to step across its line under penalty of death. The Hau-Haus proclaimed an Aukati of their own, but it was short-lived when their leader, Te Kooti, was captured and sent as a prisoner to the Chatham Islands.

Sir George next turned his attention to the loyal Maoris by conferring on them the full privileges of British citizens. A Native Rights Act endowed their land customs with the force of law, a Native Lands Act established land courts with Maori and English jurors, and in 1867 the Maori tribes were asked to elect four chiefs to represent them in the House of Representatives. Other considerations included the endowment of Maori schools. To be recognized as an equal with white settlers, to receive the same privileges, to obey the same laws and to fight under the same flag, fulfilled the hopes of all those chiefs who had sought justice. Peace should have been assured but the war dragged on for two more years beyond 1868, the year of the governor's recall to England. A victim of politics, Sir George Grey, more than any other man, had saved the new colony from collapse and had shaped its policy. Indignant protests poured into London's Colonial Office, especially from Maori chiefs who, for many years following, regarded him as their true governor and their savior.

Te Kooti, with other fanatical rebels, escaped from the Chatham Islands in a stolen government schooner. They landed in Poverty Bay where they brutally attacked the colonists, murdering many of them. This deed was followed by others just as horrible. Troops stormed Te Kooti's impregnable *pa* without success; he emerged again and again to inflict bloody war on innocent village people. At last Te Kooti and his followers were driven into the King Country where they found refuge. Only then did peace come to New Zealand. The two chiefs instrumental in bringing this about were given swords of honor and commissions as majors by Queen Victoria.

When the Maori wars ended New Zealand was left financially exhausted. The Maoris, their numbers greatly reduced since the turn of the century, were dispirited and broken. For a generation it seemed they would never revive. But their innate qualities of stamina and determination, and the kindly aid of their conquerors, the first generation of New Zealand-born Pakehas, made possible a miraculous recovery which, during the years since, has never ceased. Today both Maori and Pakeha can truly claim to be one people, New Zealanders, and racial or color problems are nearly non-existent.

9

⋀⋁⋀⋁⋀⋁

Shaping a Nation

ONLY A FEW Maoris lived in the South Island, so it was spared the devastating effects of war and, though the island chafed under the necessity of financing the North Island during the troubled years, it prospered and grew rich after gold was discovered in 1861. An important find in the Clutha Valley, near Dunedin, brought prospectors streaming into New Zealand. The population jumped from 75,000 in 1860 to 300,000 in 1870. The excitement started when a miner swam across some rapids to rescue his dog from drowning. On the point where he landed the lucky prospector washed out more than $5000 worth of gold that same day. Gold was also discovered along the west coast and by the shores of Golden Bay. Prospectors panned for the alluvial gold; later gold dredges were introduced and,

Prospectors recovering gold with a cradle and rocker on South Island's west coast are a picturesque reminder of the great gold rush of 1864-1876.

although by 1870 the richest deposits had been mined, dredges are used to this day along the west coast and on the Hauraki Peninsula in the North Island.

Wool, wheat, and gold were New Zealand's main exports—and tallow when depression years forced farmers to destroy their sheep. In the 1870s land was being opened up in the U.S.A., Canada, and Russia. Thus, competition drove prices down and hard times struck New Zealand. The depression paved the way for a political revolution brought about, quietly, by the firmly entrenched settlers who sought to destroy the upstart aristocracy of newly rich big landowners. Having come to New Zealand to escape the abuses of wealth and privilege, New Zealand's citizens were determined to avoid similar conditions in a colony that had, to some extent, been established as a social protest. They voiced their dissent by a march to the polls.

After a general election New Zealand saw a decided swing to the political left and, with John Ballance at the helm for three years, the country was launched on a long career of radical reforms. Many new laws were introduced. The large estates were made unprofitable by means of a land tax which led to their subdivision into small farms. Subsidized farmers were in a position to take advantage of the newly invented refrigeration and thus sell their produce overseas. Richard Seddon was Ballance's successor in 1893. Having won the public's popular favor as well as its confidence, he ruled New Zealand as an autocrat— but wisely. Women were given the vote. Pensions for the aged were provided by the state. The Industrial and Arbitration Act, in 1894, regulated conditions of employment; it settled disputes between employer and employee, shortened the working day, increased wages, and lengthened vacation periods. New Zealand led the world in labor-management reform. Since that revolutionary period in the 1800s political changes have been few and only at long intervals.

New Zealanders, recovering from the spiritual and economic exhaustion which had followed the long years of war between the Maoris and the Pakeha settlers, looked forward to entering the twentieth century in undisturbed peace. But in 1899 the long-brewing South African discords erupted into war. New Zealand promptly offered troops to aid Britain in the fight against the Boers. Between the start of the war and 1902, when it ended, more than 6000 mounted men volunteered for service in South Africa. The high quality of the peacetime volunteer training was reflected in the troops' adaptability to rugged fight-

ing conditions which, although foreign to them, they faced unfalteringly.

The Boer War, however, was but a prologue to the great
World War, the war that started in 1914 on the other side of
the globe. New Zealand, now an independent dominion, sent
more than 100,000 men (over 40% of those eligible in age for
service) from a total population of 1,145,000. Of this number
16,700 gave their lives in overseas service.

"All we are and all we have is at the disposal of the British
Government. . . ." The Prime Minister's impassioned words
crackled over the cables within a few minutes of Britain's decla-
ration of war on Germany in 1914. New Zealand was the first
Commonwealth member to rush to the aid of the mother country; the first Allied country to occupy enemy territory—German
West Samoa. Both Maori and Pakeha young men shouldered
arms unhesitatingly; they turned toward embattled Europe and
marched off to war. Men of the first expeditionary force to be
sent overseas took part in the Gallipoli landing, a campaign
filled with blunders and a tragic waste of manpower.

The Gallipoli Peninsula, that part of Turkey in Europe
stretching for forty miles into the Aegean Sea, is separated from
Turkey in Asia by a narrow outlet from the Sea of Marmara
called the Dardanelles. The campaign's purpose was to occupy
Constantinople, Turkey's capital (now renamed Istanbul), in
order to assure passage for Russian ships. Strategists declared
it was imperative to capture the peninsula and thereby have
control of the Dardanelles. Secretly, a vast army was trans-
ported to a point off Gallipoli's north coast. In addition to
French and British soldiers there were the untried New Zealanders and Australians. Little was known of the terrain, a bar-

ren expanse of wasteland and jagged peaks, yet in the blackness
of a cold April night a large force of infantrymen were piled
into landing boats a few miles off shore. The boats drifted
with the current in the dark so that with dawn's coming the
troops saw formidable cliffs before them rather than the expected
level ground. The dawn also brought a barrage of deadly fire
from Turkish soldiers entrenched above the cliffs. Bullets and
hand grenades rained down upon the men, animals, and stores
which were squeezed into a narrow beachhead. Hundreds of
men were struck down as they waded ashore so that within a
few minutes the water was stained with the blood of the wounded
and the dead.

In the tumult, in obedience to an order to attack, the New
Zealanders and Australians stormed the rugged, exposed precipice. They clawed and lunged and beat their way up the cliff
face and, although driven back at first, they dug in and held
on grimly. So, proving themselves to be first-caliber soldiers,
the Anzacs became famous as fighting men. New Zealand gave
the NZ to ANZAC—a word built from the initial letters of Australia New Zealand Army Corps. April 25, the date of that
landing in 1915, is Memorial Day for the two Commonwealth
nations so heroically involved. Many extraordinary acts of
courage were committed on landing day and during the months
to follow. Sometimes the Anzacs were entrenched within a few
yards of the Turks and once, during the scorching summer
when corpses were piled high between them, a truce was called.
As they worked together in digging great common graves among
the poppy-flecked fields, all animosity died between Turks and
Anzacs. A temporary camaraderie developed; the men even
exchanged gifts—Turkish fruit and candy for Anzac canned

beef and cigarettes. But this was only an interlude; the war went on.

Early in August a big attack was planned and New Zealanders were chosen to storm the highest point, Chunuk Bair, at a height of 850 feet. Two companies attacked a point directly below the summit where they waited, in shallow trenches, for reinforcements. But the New Zealanders were behind enemy lines on an open hilltop with very little cover and by night almost all had been killed, for the men were under heavy Turkish fire all through the day. After the war a tall white monument was erected on Chunuk Bair in honor of the soldiers of the New Zealand Expeditionary Force who came "from the uttermost ends of the earth."

The Gallipoli campaign dragged on for nearly eight months with no objectives won. Spasmodic outbursts of ferocious fighting alternated with periodic periods of inertia between Turk and Anzac, for both were fever-ridden, poorly rationed, and ill equipped. The evacuation was the one successful maneuver. Carried through skillfully during the nights, it was completed, on December 20, with no casualties. But the high casualty list for the whole futile campaign was staggering. More than half of all the men in action, both Turks and Allies, were on that list.

The New Zealand army, described as "that ball of fire" by Winston Churchill, went on to augment its reputation in Palestine and on the battlefields of France until World War I ended in 1918.

One English lieutenant commander, who received recognition for his brave performance during the Gallipoli landing, came to play a large part in the lives of New Zealanders. The following year he received the Victoria Cross, Britain's highest military honor. During World War II, as Lieutenant General Bernard C. Freyberg, he was in command of the New Zealand forces in Greece, Crete, North Africa, and Italy and, while in action, received two bars to his V.C. By the time General Freyberg represented the British Crown as governor general in New Zealand he was Lord Freyberg, V.C., G.C.M.G., K.C.B., C.B., K.B.E., D.S.O., LL.D., D.C.L., and was acknowledged as being one of the greatest generals of all time. General Freyberg died in 1963 in England.

In 1939, when World War II started, New Zealanders again rushed to Britain's aid. This time, to preserve their identity, New Zealand servicemen preferred to be called Kiwis. By 1942

New Zealand's famous fighting men during a break in basic training in the rough country surrounding Waiouru Military Camp.

more than 200,000 men and women were serving in some branch of the armed forces. Of this number 9000 were with the Royal Air Force in the Battle of Britain and in other theaters of war; more than one third were killed. Ships of the Royal New Zealand Navy were placed under the command of the British Admiralty. New Zealand's Navy and Air Force took part in the Pacific campaign against Japan also.

A volunteer Maori battalion, under Maori officers, lived up to tradition by fighting with courage and audacity, especially in close combat when war *hakas,* combined with bayonet charges, demoralized the enemy. One Maori officer, Lieutenant Moana-Nui-a-Kiwa Ngarimu, received the V.C. posthumously, for "most conspicuous gallantry and outstanding leadership."

New Zealand contributed two naval frigates and a special combat force, including an artillery regiment and auxiliary services, when in 1950 the United Nations called for volunteers to put down aggression in Korea.

Because New Zealand is a member of the British Commonwealth and the United Nations, and has signed treaties with Australia, the United States and the South-East Asia Treaty Organization (SEATO), a defense force must be maintained. The permanent forces are small but efficient and are trained for modern warfare. Volunteers undertake to serve, part time, for a minimum of three years. Thus, to keep the peace, New Zealand's armed forces are equipped to carry on, if necessary, as hard-fighting Kiwis.

10

/.Λ.Λ.Λ.Λ

The Maoris of Today

TAIRAWHITI, Coast of the Rising Sun, is the name given by the Maoris to the stretch of land north of Poverty Bay where Captain Cook first touched Aotearoa. It is a lovely land, occupied mainly by Maoris although open to all who wish to farm there. Recently the Minister of Maori Affairs attended a meeting in Ruatoria, a little town in Tairawhiti. Under debate was the search for the ideal word signifying unity, a word that would counteract the despised *apartheid*. Someone suggested that the expression Governor Hobson used at Waitangi be adopted: *He iwi Kotahi tatou* (Now we are one people). But as a slogan it was too long. Then a Tgati-porou tribal leader spoke up. "Shorten it to *Tatou-tatou,* meaning Us-us," he said. "It is bad English, perhaps, but very good Maori." The terse phrase is applicable, for Maori and Pakeha are united; they are one people.

Many who have since achieved renown began life in Tairawhiti. The Victoria Cross winner, his noble name Te Moana-Nui-a-Kiwa bestowed only upon those of whom valor is expected, was born near Ruatoria. George Nepia, a former rugby football player, lives near Ruatoria. Now a serious farmer, he wins awards for scientific farming.

The passing of a Maori Land Act in 1929 initiated a well-thought-out plan for developing idle Maori lands and for training farmers under government supervision and guidance. The scheme embraced not only large tracts of virgin Maori lands but also small holdings scattered throughout New Zealand. While receiving financial assistance farmers are taught the advantages of modern farming. Inspired by their natural gift for emulation, Maori farmers responded enthusiastically and, as a success, the scheme surpassed all expectations. By 1955 more than 500,000 acres were under cultivation. Every year since 1955, new land has been grassed at the rate of approximately 10,000 acres.

On the long peninsula north of Auckland, in the vicinity of sheltered bays where, perhaps, their ancestors first landed, live the greatest congregation of Maoris in New Zealand. Many Pakehas live there also, close by the first English settlement. Wearing the schools' uniforms, brown-skinned and white-skinned young people share classes in subjects that include Polynesian as well as European history. On February 6, every year, the signing of the Treaty of Waitangi is commemorated. Attending the ceremonies, on the very spot of the treaty's signing, proud Maori chiefs, clad in tribal robes of great splendor, repeat speeches that were delivered on that memorable day in 1840. Then Britain's Governor-General speaks, a sailor raises the British flag, and ships of the Royal New Zealand Navy, anchored in the Bay of Islands, fire a salute. It is a great day for New Zealanders, for the promises contained in the treaty have been fulfilled.

The attractions of urban life bring Maoris to the cities and about one quarter of their total number live in cities, particularly Auckland. Thus, more and more Maoris have been drawn into occupations and professions found only in urban areas. To help young Maoris become adapted to city and European ways, government provides specialized schools—professional, commercial, industrial. As a result of this preparation Maoris now practice as doctors and dentists, in the ministry and forestry, as mechanical and electrical engineers, as building constructors, and in every existing occupation, including politics. The girls excel in secretarial work, dressmaking, and nursing, for which they show a special aptitude. Maori women practice as doctors and dentists also, and many are in the teaching profession. The Maoris' inherited skill as craftsmen lead them into the arts; they keep alive the ancient arts of wood carving and weaving as well as achieving success in modern sculpture and painting. Their true clear voices, combined with a love of music, have produced singers of exceptional ability. In 1962 the emergence of a mezzo-soprano, Hannah Tatana, twenty-two years old, marked a milestone in Maori cultural life. Hannah carried the lead role in *Carmen* with such pronounced musical authority, power, and feeling that the critics promise her a golden future in her chosen operatic career.

Where the Waikato and Wipa rivers meet at Ngaruawahia

Maori canoe race on the Waikato River.

in the King Country, Maoris temporarily set aside their European achievements at the big annual festival; they express their talents in old ways as in the old days. Among other events, replicas of ancient canoes are pitted, one against the other, in races. Paddled with dexterity, the canoes jump hurdles, make fast turns, and swing around the hazards. How deftly the Maoris handle them! There is rarely a spill or an overturned canoe in the Maoris' obstacle race. The splashing, the shouting, the photo-finishes, bring cheers and applause from the crowds drawn irresistibly to share the exciting scene. Pakehas compete also, in sculling and speedboat racing, but nothing quite equals the enthusiasm shown for the Maori canoe races. Prominent in the audience stands the Maori King, benign, majestic, gracious; he is proud that, as in the old days, the arts and skills are handed down through the generations.

The afternoons are given over to song and dance on Ngaruawahia's common. The girls dance together; slow, graceful, intense, revolving about each other, they move their hands with the grace of birds. They introduce subtle variations of rhythm as their undulating grass skirts flow about their gently moving knees. As the dance finishes the girls sink to the ground in beautifully relaxed postures.

The onlookers move back into a closely massed circle when the men line up, their heads and chests raised proudly. Slowly at first they chant the words of battle, then a shimmer of elation flows through the performers as they dramatize the meaning of the war *haka,* stamping and shouting without interrupting the rhythm. By the time the last defiant shout ends the dance a seeming resistance against the very spirit of civilization has taken hold.

Gradually there is less dancing and more singing, low-toned. Lullabies follow tender love songs quickly, one after another. At last only the plaintive notes of *"Po Atarau,"* the "Maori Song of Farewell," are heard. Familiar to many as a popular song, few know that both words and music belong to the Maoris of New Zealand. As the sun goes down over Aotearoa they sing, in close harmony, "Now is the hour/When we must say goodby . . ."

11

/\\./\\./\\./\\.\

New Zealand's Wild Life

A LONG TIME AGO New Zealand birds led an untroubled, secure life. They felt free to fossick on the forest floor, scratching among the ferns or turning over fallen leaves as they searched for insects and worms. Until man's coming they had no natural enemies, no land mammals at all to contend with except two species of bats, and birds had no place in their diet. Gradually, many birds kept to the ground exclusively; they lost the use of their wings and became flightless birds, or ratites.

The biggest of these flightless birds were the moas and the largest of about twenty-five moa species is known to scientists as *Dinornis maximus*. It was quite the largest feathered creature ever to have stalked the earth. No white person has seen a moa, for they were hunted to death by the moa hunters, unknown predecessors of the Maoris. The bones and mummified remains of hundreds of moas have been found in limestone caves and swamps so that scientists have been able to reconstruct the bird, quite accurately, from bones and feathers. He was anything but beautiful. Although a moa attained a height of 12 feet 6 inches, his long thin neck terminated in a puny head, hardly bigger than a barnyard rooster's, while his bulky body, sparsely feathered, was supported by thick, muscular legs. What wings remained were ridiculously small in proportion to his size.

One flightless bird of only three that are still around is the kiwi, *Apteryz Australis*. It is held in high esteem by New Zealanders and, with the fern, is their country's emblem. Kiwi, the appellation adopted not only by army servicemen but by travelers abroad, is further evidence of their affection for this

New Zealand's unique Kiwi.

unique bird, so elusive and so shy. Scientists back in England a hundred and fifty years ago cried, "Impossible!" when given a description of a kiwi, for this improbable bird has no outward sign of wing or tail, its feathers resemble brownish hair, and it has whiskers like a cat. Slightly larger than a farm hen, the kiwi lays an enormous egg, weighing a quarter of its own weight, which, for egg-laying records, puts the moa to shame: his egg was only one and a half times larger. If the kiwi's distant relative, the ostrich, laid an egg of comparable size it would weigh seventy-five pounds. The kiwi's sensitive bill is a real working tool, measuring five inches and, contrary to bird rule, with nostrils at the tip rather than the base. The bill is useful in smelling out and digging deep down for fat worms for which the kiwi has an insatiable appetite, consuming five or six hundred daily. The kiwi is nocturnal, has poor eyesight but keen hearing, a possible reason why so few New Zealanders have actually seen a kiwi in its wild state. But the kiwi can be heard, on a still night, whistling "kee-wee" as it scampers through the debris in the woods. The male kiwi builds the nest and for eighty days sits, facing south, on the one or, very rarely, two eggs. During this trying ordeal he is apt to lose one third or more of his weight. Kiwi remains have been found at depths of seventy feet; they have inhabited New Zealand since prehistoric times. Since man's comparatively recent arrival, however, more changes have occurred in New Zealand's natural life than, probably, for a million years. The kiwi was marked for extinction when the early settlers found it made a tasty pie and its hollow legs were good as pipestems; the Maoris found its hairy feathers a satisfactory trimming for their capes. Now, kiwis are closely protected, both in their wild state and in zoos.

As recently as 1948 the rediscovery of another flightless bird, the takahe, made the headlines in London's newspapers; it brought acclaim from ornithologists and bird lovers all over the world. Takahes had not been seen since 1898 and it was presumed that they were no more, but after a persistent, thirty-year-long search, Dr. G. B. Orbell, a South Island physician, found takahes in the high valleys above Fiordland. Now takahes, although their territory has been declared a sanctuary, have been photographed discreetly, and filmed. Experts study their habits through field glasses; they see them sliding their heavy, scarlet bills down the tall grass stems, snipping off the seeds as their bills progress. Heavy legs match a takahe's bill in color and a gorgeous peacock-blue cape, merging into pea green, makes the takahe a photogenic beauty.

Birds of the air are as colorful as they are varied in New Zealand. The woods are filled with flycatchers and honey eaters, their exquisite songs accompanied by the squawks and hoots of parrots and owls indigenous to New Zealand. One parrot, the kea, has proved himself a real villain. In the early days of Pakeha settlement sheep farmers shook their heads and pondered. What strange disease of the kidneys was killing their sheep? Then the keas were seen swooping down from rocky mountain crags upon the defenseless sheep. Being pretty smart birds, they were quick to learn that a morsel of kidney fat was the tastiest dinner a kea could wish for. A bounty has been placed on keas, but whenever those bold birds find a chance, they still pounce on helpless sheep.

New Zealand is enriched with an abundance of sea birds. In springtime there is barely enough room for the nests of petrels, shags, gannets, gulls, godwits, and terns that crowd the

(Above) *A blue penguin and* (Below) *a colony of gannets.*

rocky cliffs and shore lines. Even the wandering albatross is pressed for space for, contrary to the general practice, New Zealand's albatross, with its nine-foot wingspread, nests on shore near Dunedin. Little blue penguins, indigenous to New Zealand's waters, frolic inshore and, like the albatross, prefer nesting in burrows, caves, even under the porches of summer baches, rather than in rookeries. Many migratory birds make New Zealand their terminal after a long, long flight from Siberia. And two species of cuckoo, the long-tailed and the shining, reappear in springtime from Polynesian islands. One touch of autumn and the migratory birds take off again.

Two factors contribute to the disappearance of New Zealand's land birds—the clearing of the forests and the introduction of mammals. When rabbits were turned loose to forage they refused, at first, to become acclimatized. The early settlers persevered, however, and as more land was cleared for pasture the rabbits began to multiply. By 1870 they were New Zealand's enemy number one, destroying crops and pastureland. Although rabbit skins were remunerative and 33,000 were exported in 1873, the number exported had increased to nearly 1,000,000 by 1882. The perplexed farmers brought in weasels, stoats, and ferrets to combat the rabbit plague. These little animals, instead, preyed upon New Zealand's flightless birds. Along with cats and dogs they almost succeeded in clearing the land of New Zealand's priceless heritage of unique birds. The war against rabbits continues. Although within ten recent years an average of 13,335,000 skins was exported, their value was no balance to the destruction caused by burrowing and overgrazing. One man put into practice his idea of dropping poisoned carrots from airplanes. After the sheep are brought from high places, flyers scatter their bait. As a result of this experiment some farmers have been able to reclaim their pasturelands and double their flocks.

The guilty role played by dogs in destroying New Zealand's indigenous birds has been forgiven, for they were invaluable aids in opening up the South Canterbury area. Without the help of these intelligent, specially bred sheep dogs, farming in the more inaccessible rockbound mountains and ravines would have been impossible. With the sanction of the Mackenzie Country Historical Society a monument, taking the form of a boundary dog sitting on top of a kennel, is being erected to the memory of all pioneer sheep dogs at Dog Kennel Corner. The Mackenzie Country acquired its name through the notorious behavior of a man named Mackenzie and his dog. He was a clever sheep stealer who lifted sheep from the Canterbury Plains to sell them far enough away to avoid suspicion. Mackenzie trained Jock, his dog, to open gates at night, drive stolen sheep along upland trails and through valleys never before visited by other men. Finally Mackenzie was caught and sent to jail. And Jock? He was tried, found guilty, and destroyed. Some people say he was hanged.

As the big farms prospered, New Zealand's citizens relaxed. Their thoughts turned to sport and hunting; they imported deer of all types—red, fallow, wapiti, Virginian, sambar, Javan rusa, Japanese, Himalayan tahr, and Austrian chamois. Today an open season prevails on deer for, like every other creature imported to New Zealand, their size and numbers outstrip performances in their native countries. As part of their training, soldiers go deer-culling to help the New Zealand Forest Service. Four-man parties learn bushcraft, marksmanship, map reading, and observation under a non-commissioned officer as they stalk mountainous, forested country in search of what are classed as noxious animals. An all-out campaign to exterminate deer is in progress; professional hunters, employed by government, bag an average of 60,000 deer annually. An equal number fall to the rifles of amateurs who need no hunting license to help put down the menace. Descendants of Captain Cook's pigs trample the woods; wild goats, Australian wallabies, and opposums create terrific havoc also.

Part of the damage done by these imported pests is the destruction of many of the 2500 indigenous plants. The chamois goat is the culprit who thins the subalpine flowering shrubs skirting mountain timber lines. These shrubs still present a colorful barrier, however, below the alpine meadows. Covering the meadows, in summer, masses of alpine flowers bloom in profusion. Dominant among the daisies, gentians, forget-me-nots, and giant edelweiss is the world's largest buttercup, the Mount Cook lily. Each plant carries twenty snow-white flowers, three inches across; its glossy leaves measure a foot or more. Lower down on the mountains and throughout both islands, one flowering shrub, manuka, spreads its flower masses, ranging in color from a silvery white to deep crimson. Manuka is useful in controlling erosion and in acting as a seedbed for New Zealand's forest trees. In the forests six varieties of clematis trail and sway from the tall trees, only superseded in beauty by some of the trees themselves. One tree, the rata, mantles itself with brilliant crimson flowers long before it reaches its majestic hundred-foot height. For golden beauty, pride of place goes to the kowhai, a member of the pea family. A hillside favored by the forty-foot high kowhais in full bloom resembles a burst of dazzling sunlight.

(Left) *Mountain Lily,* Ranunculus Godleyanus. (Right) *Mountain Daisy,* Celmisia.

. . . Spring wakes our Lovely Lady of the Bush,
The Kowhai; and she hastes to wrap herself
All in a mantle wrought of living gold. . . .

The pohutukawa, meaning spray-sprinkled, is one of New Zealand's loveliest flowering trees. No doubt the appropriate Maori name refers to the silvery undersides of its deep green leaves which, when tossed by winds, flicker like whitecaps. Pohutukawas cling to cliff faces along the coast for preference, but they are also found inland. Profuse scarlet blossoms burst into full bloom in mid-December; this beauty comes as a delightful Christmas present to Pakeha New Zealanders who commonly call pohutukawas the Christmas tree.

In the middle of this congestion of flowering shrubs and trees, undisturbed by hunted deer and those who hunt them, about 100,000 glowworms cast their blue light in the quiet and calm of Waitomo Grotto. *Arachnocampa luminosa* inhabits damp, shady caves and crevices throughout New Zealand. In the Waitomo Caves the glowworms have found the ideal environment, breeding so prolifically that they must fight for space on the high, domed ceiling. Visitors find it ideal also, for a lazy river flows through the grotto and from a boat, which a guide propels by an overhead wire, they can look up to the galaxy of twinkling lights above them. Make a sound and the glowworms put out their lights, but the guide's warning is hardly necessary; visitors are awed into speechlessness. A 52° temperature and the right humidity are unvarying in the grotto, which is 100 feet long and 40 feet wide. Midges, which breed in the water, are the glowworms' staple diet. The hungrier a glowworm is the brighter his light, enticing the prey to its dozen or more ingenious "fishlines" baited with glistening drops of mucus. When it senses a catch the glowworm draws in the line, consuming both it and the fly as he does so. This insect, quite unlike the Northern Hemisphere's phosphorescent beetle, fulfills its life history in four stages—egg, larva, pupa, and adult fly. After about four weeks tiny larvae are hatched from eggs, which immediately emit a piercing greenish-blue light while lowering their lines. Over several months they grow to about one and a half inches in length, when they shed their larval skin and become pupae. A complete change transpires within the pupae, or chrysalises, before they emerge, after twelve days, as adult flies. The life cycle of the glowworm is continuous, so that this brilliant manifestation of nature can be enjoyed throughout the year, providing excitement and never-to-be-forgotten memories for the 90,000 visitors who annually come to share the marvels

Glowworms illuminate ceiling of Waitomo Cave. Insert shows glowworm in pupal stage. Fly will emerge from this chrysalis, to live just long enough to lay eggs, renewing the eternal cycle.

of Waitomo Grotto.

New Zealand is singularly free from noxious insects. One spider only, the katipo, is poisonous and it chooses the reeds by remote seashores as its domicile. And a stroller through the bushland has no need to watch the trail; of poisonous snakes there are none.

Leaving the mainland, one finds a strange domestic arrangement on some of New Zealand's cool, foggy offshore islands. Lizards and petrels share burrows. The tuatara, or *Sphenodon punctatum,* is the sole survivor of a lizard species from prehistoric days. It once lived on the mainland, but those imported pests quickly exterminated it. Now tuatara has adapted itself to living out its hundred-year-long life span in temperatures so low that other reptiles would be stiff and immovable. Grayish black, spiny, and about eighteen inches long, the tuatara once possessed a third, pineal eye, now covered with a scaly skin. Lethargic in its movements, a tuatara is also nocturnal—and lazy, so lazy that he won't build a burrow for himself. Sharing a petrel's burrow works out very well, for petrels, being migratory birds, leave the tuatara in charge for six months. Discord occurs only at nesting time when an irate male petrel sometimes tosses tuatara outside. Then, with hurt feelings, he scurries around in search of another burrow he can move into. Petrels, or sooty shearwaters, are preserved in perpetuity for the Maoris since chiefs sold Steward Island to the government for $18,000 in 1840. The young petrels, called muttonbirds by Maoris, are a delicacy that they catch by hand, then salt down in barrels.

On New Zealand's surrounding seas one occasionally sees dolphins and seals, now rigidly protected, but one hears the story of Pelorus Jack, the individualistic, solitary white dolphin that used to pilot coastal vessels through parts of Cook Strait. For longer than fifty years Jack brought delight to passengers who made the trip, many times, solely for the purpose of seeing him. "Here he comes," they would shout as they strained to see the great cetacean leaping through the waves or frolicking off the ship's bow. Requests to be called when Jack appeared brought overnight travelers bounding on deck to catch a glimpse of the silvery shape, shimmering in phosphorescent white, as he flashed by the ship. He was given the scientific name Risso's dolphin (*Grampus griseus*) in 1904 and proclaimed as protected under order-in-council of the New Zealand Government. No gun or harpoon could destroy him. But in 1912 Jack disappeared. Whether he was shot or harpooned or just died of old age remains a mystery to this day.

A wealth of Maori folklore surrounds Pelorus Jack. He was the reincarnation of one tribe's sea god, Koukai-a-waro. Twelve generations ago, or three hundred years, he adopted Matua-hautere and his tribe when they came seeking a refuge in South Island bays. The sea god performed miraculous acts on their behalf. He nosed out a channel where a river now flows; he saw them settled safely before he returned to the cave where he lived. When his protégés fished for hapuku or rock cod he escorted them, leading them to the richest fishing grounds. All he asked in return were a few fish scraps. One time Koangaumu, a descendant chief of that same tribe, was captured by enemies. He and his companions were imprisoned on an island, but during the night they built a raft of flax and reeds and, disregarding storm clouds, set off for home. A great storm arose, lightning flashed around them, huge waves threatened to overturn the flimsy craft. In dire need, Koangaumu prayed to his sea god, his *taniwha,* for help. The good sea god heard. Leaving his cave, he skimmed over the angry waves to the frail craft, which was breaking up and sinking. Commanding a calm passage, he led them safely home. What a comfort it must have been, in those bygone days, to have had such a protector!

12

/\/\/\/\/\

New Zealanders at Work

As IN ALL newly settled countries, the first articles to be manufactured in New Zealand were for meeting the needs of the people—clothing, building materials, ropes and spars for ships—but as communications were made easier by improved roads, opportunities opened up for factory expansion. World War II stimulated the manufacture of goods that could no longer be imported. Truck gardens were started in order to feed the thousands of men in the United States forces. Now the largest industrial group is that engaged in food processing, for more than 10,000,000 pounds of canned and frozen vegetables are exported every year. Although about 12% of the entire labor force is employed by government, 226,000 persons are employed in 20,000 factories making a wide variety of articles.

112

Hauling the catch on board. One crayfish is escaping.

Many kinds of fruits, such as grapes, berries, citrus fruits, peaches, and pears flourish in New Zealand, but apples account for over half the total orchard area. In one year 70,500,000 pounds of apples, valued at $6,100,000, were exported. Smoked or frozen eels and fish, blue cheese, frozen vegetables, and fresh fruits are exported to Australia in large quantities. Goat meat goes to the West Indies, canned, curried mutton to Jamaica, and ice cream mixes find a ready market in tropical New Guinea. A demand for cookies, which have sweet butter as an ingredient rather than inferior oils and fats, are popular exports also. The United States buys approximately 900 tons of frozen crayfish tails every year, for America, after Great Britain, is New Zealand's best customer for all exports.

In a season that lasts from February to November nine huge dredges comb the ocean floor with steel nets for oysters that are found in Foveaux Strait, which separates the South Island from Stewart Island. The men employed in opening the catch receive about five cents a dozen, but as the average number opened by each is 600 dozen daily their incomes are fairly sub-

stantial. These large succulent oysters are canned but not exported. Bivalves called toheroas (meaning long-tongue) are unique to New Zealand. They are found buried beneath the sand along the beaches of the North Island's west shore where the tide recedes two hundred yards. Their food is plankton, a marine organism blown in by the prevailing west winds, which give these shellfish a delicate flavor and greenish color. The oil from ships wrecked in World War II and auto racing along the beaches threatened toheroas with extinction; now their harvesting is limited to twenty for each casual digger. But a nearby cannery makes toheroa soup which is relished by gourmets everywhere. Another remunerative industry is the making of a pure beer, free from preservatives or added carbonic acid gas. Brewed in 50,000-gallon vats, its contents are malt, yeast, water, and hops from South Island hop fields. New Zealand beer ranks with the best because of its purity; it wins medals at international exhibitions. These are but a few foods grown and processed for export from New Zealand. A Virginia-type tobacco is imported, but seven factories use 35% of New Zealand-grown tobacco in the manufacture of their 7,075,577-pound seasonal production. As a new enterprise, home-grown tobacco's output is steadily increasing.

Indigenous flax, now grown commercially on farms, thrives in swamplands and the long, sword-shaped leaves are processed and manufactured into wool baling, upholsterers' hemp, and floor matting. The U. S. Navy used flax cordage in large quantities during World War II. The strength and durability of New Zealand flax is such that other countries now import its seed.

Another unique yield from New Zealand's soil is kauri gum,

an everlasting substance dug at depths varying from a few inches to twenty feet. At one time Dalmatians came to New Zealand to dig kauri gum for use in varnishes and to carve as ornaments. Over the years more than $100,000,000 worth of the amberlike resin has been exported. Today, because of the invention of synthetic materials, the industry is less active. However, about 200 tons of gum are still dug out every year.

The principal ports for loading New Zealand's exports are, in the North Island, Auckland, Wellington, and Tauranga, a newly developed harbor on the Bay of Plenty, convenient for handling wood pulp and paper products. In the South Island the main ports are Lyttelton, Dunedin, and Timaru, which has an artificial harbor that is enclosed within two man-made moles, or breakwaters, 3000 by 2000 feet. Timaru Harbor was commenced in 1870 and completed in 1907. A new train ferry across Cook Strait speeds the interchange of commerce between the two islands. The South Island sends north for its fruit while the North Island is dependent upon the South Island for its bread. Wheat is New Zealand's main grain crop and most of this is grown on the Canterbury Plains. Large quantities of seed peas, grass, and clover seeds are exported to Britain, Australia, and the United States.

New Zealand is less generous in her yield of minerals. Except for gold and coal, few minerals of great economic value have been discovered. Gold mining on a large scale belongs to the past, although along the western coastline the dark sands hold gold and other minerals, such as iron, brought down by swift-flowing rivers and pounded by heavy seas into tiny particles. As yet no method of extracting this wealth has been found. Government owns and operates thirteen opencast coal mines that annually produce 888,000 tons of four types of coal. Only a little silver is mined; other ores, such as antimony, arsenic, copper, tungsten, and manganese, are in small quantities also, or they lie in inaccessible areas. Oil has been discovered but it, too, is in negligible amounts.

Heavy industry is limited to railroad workshops, fertilizer, and cement machinery production because of the scarcity of iron, but light-metal industries have made prodigious strides during the postwar years. All household electrical appliances, television and radio equipment, automobile parts, and small machines are made locally. Textiles are important to New Zealand's economy. Yard goods are manufactured from her fine merino wools and made into quality blankets and clothing. Combined with leather trimmings, made supple and silky by careful processing, New Zealand's women's fashions more than hold their own in competitive markets. Hides, pelts, and skins to the value of $36,000,000 are exported every year, but many leather goods are manufactured in New Zealand. Leather upholstery, saddles, and handbags are locally made; mountain climbers, deerstalkers, and New Zealand army men march in leather boots that have been rigidly tested by the New Zealand Leather and Shoe Association.

Perhaps New Zealand's greatest wealth of all, however, lies in her dense quiet forests which cover one fourth of the land, in the rich potentialities of timber's many ramifications—the paper for book publishing, the boards for building, the newsprint for daily newspapers—from the biggest man-planted forests in the world.

13
/\.\/\.\/\.\

Mother Earth
and Father Sky

BEFORE time began, one poetic yet sad Maori myth explains, Rangi, the Sky Father, and Papa, the Earth Mother, were wedded. In darkness they lay close together, for there was no light. Their one son, Tane, had many children who became the tall trees festooned with clematis, the stout rata, thorny lawyer vines, and lush ferns that crowd the forest floors. These restless children strived to separate Rangi and Papa by pushing toward the sky in an effort to find light. Thus the Sky Father was driven upward and the children gained freedom to move and spread upon the breast of Papa, the Earth Mother. But forever afterward the grandparents lamented. Rangi lets fall his lonely tears as rain or silent dew; sometimes, in despair,

117

he sends winds to buffet the children and force them from Papa, but the wind only makes the children cling more tightly together; they regard it as their common enemy. "Leave them to me," Earth Mother says when the strong winds blow. "They have rebelled against us, but they are Tane's children." Then she gathers them to her, but, in sadness, she demonstrates her love for Rangi by making the mists rise softly and quietly.

First the Maoris brushed aside, unthinkingly, Tane's children. They tore away large chunks of forestland and replaced it with farms and pastures. Then came the European settlers. In their eagerness to become established they ruthlessly cut and milled New Zealand's timber. They burned and cleared the woods indiscriminately until timber resources were reduced to almost nothing. Sometimes the early settlers have been called the early vandals because of their thoughtless destruction, which threatened the land with erosion and, in some areas, absolutely demolished the forests. The kauri forests alone were reduced from 2,000,000 to 25,000 acres. This remnant is now preserved in the Waipoua State Forest in Northland where trees of great antiquity and majesty are known, individually, by name. "Tanemahuta," a giant among other mighty kauris, deserves its title as Father of the Forest.

Scientists from the New Zealand Forest Service eyed the widespread barren lands with apprehension, then they focused their attention on the North Island's central plain; it gave promise as a possible site for a tree-planting program that would more than recover the lost timberlands. Geological ages ago volcanoes, now extinct, had showered soft volcanic rock and pumice untold fathoms deep over the plain. Then, as recently as 1886, Mount Tarawera, 3646 feet in height and one of the last active

Pinus Radiata forest near Rotorua, North Island.

volcanoes, erupted violently, buried a Maori village, destroyed itself but spread sand widely over the undulating countryside, thus creating perfect conditions for fast-growing softwoods.

Although the varieties of pines and beeches endemic to New Zealand number more than 112, they are, on the whole, slow growing. It was necessary to look for a variety of pine that would adapt to New Zealand's soil and climate. After careful, cautious experimentation, *Pinus radiata* was found to respond most quickly in growth and was ideal as a source of raw material for pulp and paper industries important to New Zealand's economy. In its native environment of California, *Pinus radiata* has reached a height of 115 feet, but in New Zealand heights of 160 feet and over are not uncommon, with diameters of more than 5 feet. It grows five times as fast as in California. *Pinus radiata* is the world's most rapid grower; in New Zealand as much as eight feet in vertical growth has been recorded for one year. It was chosen as the principal timber species for the tree-planting program started in the 1920s.

Thirty years later 220,000,000 trees covered 1,000,000 acres of private and state-owned forests growing at the rate of 10,000 tons of timber a day. But the Kaingaroa State Forest, in the center of the North Island, covers the widest area. Kaingaroa yields its timber wealth on an everlasting basis, for as each block of trees is cut out new trees are planted. This ever expanding enterprise, when viewed from a nearby mountaintop, appears in rows like roller-coaster tracks, rising and falling over the hills to lose themselves in distance. These square miles covered with green-pointed pines are cared for by eight permanently manned fire towers that rise above the treetops. By radio, watchers are capable of giving split-second warning of fire threats; radio-equipped aircraft patrol the area and pilots are trained to direct fire-fighting operations from the air. Periodic fire drills are constantly revised and improved upon, campers and picnickers are forbidden to trespass, and 800 miles of roads and firebreaks give extra close-range access. A Forest Biology Survey keeps a watch for insect attacks or fungus growth and, as a further precaution, the forest floor is kept cleared of scrub and decaying wood, their possible breeding places. As a consequence, Kaingaroa is singularly free from insect pests.

Miles of logs roll on specially built railroads from Kaingaroa to where modern mills have been built. Timber milling on a large scale is conducted in three integrated plants producing timber, pulp, paper, and board. One of the three plants,

Kawerau (meaning Countless Carriers), stands in a new thriving town of that name by the Tarawera River. American and English engineers, Scots, Dutch, and Danish construction workers, Finnish pulp workers, Canadian loggers, and Australian carpenters make Kawarau an international town where children of thirteen nationalities attend the grade and high schools.

The plant's sawmill is the largest in the Southern hemisphere and the newsprint machine is the fourth largest in the world. A 50-mile-long railroad brings the logs into the mill's stockpile, then carries the processed products on to Tauranga Harbor where deep-sea wharves can handle three oceangoing freighters at once. Kawerau's output is 75,000 tons of newsprint, 40,000 tons of wood pulp and 72,000,000 board feet of sawn timber every year. Before too long, these figures will be doubled.

New Zealand is a world leader in timber preservation for, after close scientific research, methods of impregnating non-durable softwoods with preservatives, such as boron followed by oil, turns them into hard durable timbers suitable for railroad ties, power poles, and other uses requiring permanency.

The mill's water supply, drawn from Mount Tarawera's barren slopes, is rich in silica, but an unexpected economy, not envisaged in the original plan, is the introduction of geothermal steam. Kawerau is located on the rim of the North Island's thermal regions where, deep down in the earth's interior, seeping water is subjected to tremendous pressures. This subterranean power has been tapped by the sinking of bores; superheated steam now kiln-dries the timber mill's output. In time it will supply all the heat, power, and light needed by both industrial and residential Kawerau.

From timber and its by-products has sprung the largest single industry ever to be established in New Zealand. Not only are paper pulp and newsprint important exports to Australia and the Far East, but their availability has acted as an incentive to home productivity. A catalogue of New Zealand books in print, issued in 1961, lists twice as many as in 1957.

Geothermal steam, drawn from the same source as that in Kawerau, is used to generate electricity at Wairakei in the thermal regions, where fifty bores are sunk to depths varying from 570 to 4000 feet. At first the roar from steam escaping into the atmosphere was so deafening to workers on the site that it was essential to find a means of reducing the overwhelming thunder. The problem was solved by a series of concrete pipes, of decreasing dimensions, leading from the outlets to the powerhouse. A water and steam separator silencer was developed also. This vast geothermal-electric project, first of its

Glass-and-aluminum power-house for the first stage of development at the Wairakei geothermal-electric project.

kind in the British Commonwealth of Nations and second in the world, drives the turbines in a new powerhouse generating 80,070 kilowatts. Building is still in progress at Wairakei where the output is planned, eventually, to produce 250,000 kilowatts.

But with its ample supply of water power, the supply of electricity offers no problem to New Zealand. About 95% of the country's power is derived from hydroelectric dams. Over the total length of the swift-flowing Waikato River seven stations now operate and plans are under consideration for three more. Several concrete dams across the South Island's rivers, fed by the Southern Alps, raise the hydraulic level sufficiently to generate enough power to supply even the remotest outposts with electricity. Now the biggest earth dam in the Southern Hemisphere is under construction. Known as the Benmore Project, the dam will rise 360 feet high, be 3000 feet long, and require 17,000,000 square yards of material. Its output is expected to reach 540,000 kilowatts.

With the availability of such an abundance of inexpensive power it is no wonder that New Zealand homes are generously equipped with electrical appliances and that New Zealanders themselves are "electricity-conscious."

14
/\.\/\\./\\.\/\\\

The Thermal Regions

THE WAIRAKEI PROJECT occupies only one small portion of the thermal regions, which extend for a hundred miles north from Lake Taupo with a width of thirty miles. A subterranean belt connects the region, geologically, with distant active volcanoes and, because it is part of the general Pacific fault system, a weakness in rock structure exists all along the line. Water from Lake Taupo percolates into this stratum of volcanic rock, is heated, expands, then is forced to the surface as geysers, hot springs, pools, and streams. The results present a multitude of spectacles as varied as New Zealand itself. Where there is pumice, boiling water and gases are expelled in loud plop, plop-plops. Pumice pools are commonly called porridge pots, a fitting appellation, for those are what they resemble. Where min-

Rangi, world-famous guide, at Pohutu Geyser, Whakarewarewa.

erals fill the water brilliant colors result. For instance, the Claret Cup lies beside the Emerald Pool. In some areas millions of gallons of water are ejected every day so that swimming pools have been built, with varying temperatures, at intervals along one stream's tumbling journey from its source to the roaring Waikato River. The Fairy Bath, in a rustic setting, is fringed with lacy ferns; a swimmer plunging through the tepid waters of a waterfall is rewarded with a view of a myriad tiny blue wild flowers hidden behind the cascade. The steam from the hot pools condenses as it meets the cooler outside air and seeps into the heated rocks again, thus completing the cycle.

The town of Rotorua is the thermal region's true center. Rotorua was recently declared a city with appropriate celebrations that lasted for a year from the date of its inauguration, April 27, 1962. In Rotorua's Geyser Valley geysers leap 100 feet skyward, and one, pushed by the tremendous force behind it, periodically shifts a rock sideways. The town includes two Maori villages, Ohinimutu and Whakarewarewa, which still follow traditional Maori customs. In these villages native clothing is worn and women prepare kumaras, with mussels, in woven containers before cooking them in the boiling pools; small boys exhibit their diving prowess by retrieving pennies shined and polished by the mineralized water. Ankle-high scars from scalding water can sometimes be seen when a miscalculation of a pool's temperature has caused a misstep, for often a thin rock ledge is all that separates a boiling-hot from an icy-cold pool. Near Rotorua deft fishermen can hook a trout in a cold stream and, with a flip of the line, plunge it into an adjacent cook pot.

In Ohinimutu and Whakarewarewa everything is carried on as it was in the early days except the fine old game of fighting. On special occasions ancient dances are performed to accompanying songs; the art of carving has been restored. The principal motifs decorating one elaborately carved gateway are the embracing figures of Hinemoa and Tutanekei, Maori history's favorite hero and heroine whose descendants still live on an island, Mokoia, that lies seemingly suspended above the shining, calm waters of Lake Rotorua.

Hinemoa was the second daughter of Umukaria, a great chief of noble lineage whose territory lay on the mainland. She was renowned for her beauty and mild, reserved bearing. Many chiefs came from far and wide to court the maid of Rotorua, but her parents guarded her as they might some rare, cherished jewel.

Tutanekai was the fourth and illegitimate son of Whakane, chief of Mokoia Island. His three brothers were fierce, strong men, fearless in battle but jealous and scornful of their young half brother who was as handsome as Hinemoa was fair; he was one, also, who preferred dabbling in music to fighting.

On one of the frequent occasions when an assembly of the tribes gathered at Chief Umukaria's *pa,* Tutanekai and Hinemoa met and, after one quick glance, fell in love. As the four brothers paddled toward their island home after one gathering the eldest inquired of the others, "Which of you pressed the hand of Hinemoa?" The second, then the third brother answered, "I pressed the hand of Hinemoa." Then they turned to Tutanekai. "Did you press the hand of Hinemoa?" they asked him. "Indeed I did," he answered proudly, "and she pressed mine in return." Now hand pressing in the early days was the gesture of affection and esteem, so the brothers scoffed at Tutanekai and taunted him. "Nonsense!" they exclaimed in chorus. "She would not press the hand of an unimportant nobody like you."

Hinemoa's parents suspected in which direction lay her affections; after that night they kept the young lovers separated. Hinemoa was never allowed to be alone, not even at night, for her sister and one handmaiden guarded her *whare* door. However, Tutanekai was able to send her a message. "When you hear music from my master's balcony," whispered the servant, "seize a canoe and paddle across the lake to Mokoia. Tutanekai will be waiting."

For many nights Hinemoa listened to the flute's beckoning call which wafted across the still waters of Lake Rotorua, but no opportunity opened for her to follow Tutanekai's plan until one dark night when both guardians slept. She stepped boldly over their bodies and ran to the shore. Every canoe had been hauled high above the water, but Hinemoa collected six large gourds and with three on each side of her she launched herself into Lake Rotorua's deep water and, with easy strokes, swam toward the island. When Hinemoa tired the gourds held her up as she floated and listened for the flute's guiding call.

Hinemoa reached Mokoia Island close to a warm spring in which she relaxed, for the long swim had set her limbs to shivering. The flute's call was very close as she hid, from shyness, and waited. Presently Tutanekai became thirsty so he called to a servant, "Fetch me water to quench my thirst so that I may continue to make music with my flute." The servant ran with a calabash to the spring but, when he stooped to fill it, a deep voice inquired, "For whom is that water?" "It is for my master, Tutanekai," answered the servant. "Well, give it to me," demanded the voice. Hinemoa took the calabash and crashed it against the rocks. When the servant returned empty-handed, Tutanekai asked, "Where is my calabash?" and the servant replied, "The man in the spring broke it." "Take another calabash and fetch me water, for I am thirsty," ordered Tutanekai. Again Hinemoa took the calabash and broke it. This incident between Hinemoa and the servant was repeated a half dozen times until Tutanekai himself stamped down to the spring. "Come out, you rogue," he called. But Hinemoa remained silent and hidden beneath an overhanging ledge. "Where are you? Come out and fight like a man," Tutanekai kept repeating. Then as a full moon rose he saw one pale hand clinging to the ledge. Seizing the hand, he drew from the water the gleaming form of his beloved. "Why, Hinemoa!" he exclaimed. "You have heeded the flute's call!" Then he wrapped his cloak around her and led her to his *whare*.

Next morning Whakane, the father, looked about him. "Where is Tutanekai? Is the lad sick?" he asked. "Go fetch him," he ordered. But the servant came running back shouting, "Master, master, I saw *four* feet in Tutanekai's house." Then all the villagers rushed to see whom Tutanekai had taken as a wife. When it was found that Hinemoa was Tutanekai's chosen bride the people rejoiced. "Welcome, Hinemoa, to Mokoia!" was everyone's cry. After that Whakane's and Umukaria's tribes were strongly united and, to this day, they never tire of telling, nor visitors of listening to, the romance of Hinemoa and Tutanekai.

Over the generations the Maori tribes became accustomed to their country's freakish behavior, for when subterranean pressures find no ready outlet through the earth's outer crust, New Zealand is subject to earthquakes; these, fortunately, are mild and infrequent. Since 1849 the death toll has been 284 and of this number 255 lost their lives in one serious 'quake in Napier on Hawke Bay, in 1931. At that time the harbor bed rose five feet; what remained of Napier after the flood was leveled by fire. But, undaunted, Napier recovered to be rebuilt with a garden-flanked Marine Parade two miles long, with sport arenas, skating rinks, and an open-air concert bowl, all of which hide earthquake scars from Napier's disaster. It is now one of the prettiest towns in New Zealand.

Far out at sea from the Bay of Plenty, volcanic White Island is in constant eruption; south of Lake Taupo one of the lake's three sentinel mountains, Ngauruhoe, lets loose with fiery foun-

Thermal activity in the crater of this volcano on White Island is awe-inspiring.

tains of white-hot rocks and molten lava. In 1953, Mount Ruapehu, one of the three, broke the bounds of its Crater Lake and swept away a bridge when, alas, a train was crossing it. These few examples of nature's forces in action, however, are regarded as New Zealand's safety valves. Undisturbed, life moves serenely forward; Rotorua's burbling pools are used as health-giving spas by many enthusiastic visitors, Mount Ngauruhoe's eruptions are viewed with wonder and delight from nearby Mount Tongariro, and skiers swim in the warm waters of Mount Ruapehu's Crater Lake.

15

/\./\./\./\./\.

New Zealanders at Play

NEW ZEALAND'S rich endowment of open-air attractions has
bred in her people more than the usual enthusiasm for recrea-
tion. All year round, over the long weekends, the great outdoors tempt New Zealanders to share in a diversity of sports—
either as participants or merely adding their cheers as spectators.

Tongariro National Park, covering 161,500 acres, is one of
nine national parks, or reserves, in New Zealand. It is the North
Island's most popular play area, with ski tows that carry de-
votees to ski slopes and mountain summits. It is there that
venturers into Crater Lake have the unique experience of swimming in a warm bath whose waters lap the crater's icy walls.

The peaks and sheer cliffs of the Southern Alps challenge
New Zealand's climbers. Alpine and mountaineering huts are

Skiers in New Zealand's Southern Alps.

conveniently spaced for the legion of ski runners and climbers who explore glaciers and mountains previously unscaled. Among both mountain and forest areas hiking is a popular pastime, also. Groups of hardy hikers, led by experienced guides, explore and penetrate into remote corners of both islands. Perhaps the favorite walk is that which ends in Milford Sound. This well-trodden trail has hikers bushwhacking through ancient forests, wading rivers, crunching across glaciers, and skirting lakes. It takes stamina and endurance for a pack-laden hiker to cover this thirty-three-mile stretch unfalteringly. Many organized gun clubs take their members on expeditions after deer, chamois, and wapiti in the bush country, for game birds, such as duck and geese, through the lake districts.

In the summertime Lake Taupo, resting on a white pumice bed, is the mecca for fishermen. Some use wet or dry spinners, others merely troll. Lake Taupo, with its adjacent streams, is famous for the quantity and size of its fish. British brown trout and California (steelhead) trout were introduced in 1895 and have, like *Pinus radiata,* multiplied and surpassed growth performances in their native countries. Twelve-pound trout are not uncommon, and it is claimed that more five- to ten-pound rainbow trout are caught in New Zealand lakes and streams than in the rest of the world put together. In some districts, law demands that any trout measuring less than fourteen inches must be returned to the water. Quinnat salmon were imported from Canada at the same time as trout were introduced. They thrive best in South Island rivers where they swim in from the sea to spawn when four years old. Anglers cast with rods using brass wobblers to catch quinnat salmon that weigh up to forty pounds. All rivers, streams, and lakes throughout New Zealand teem with fish; in places there seem to be almost more fish than water, making it truly the fisherman's paradise.

However, for real fishing thrills, nothing quite compares with New Zealand's big game fishing. Zane Grey, the American novelist, brought fame to the warm, sheltered waters off Whangaroa after he wrote *Tales of an Angler's Eldorado* in 1925. When he took the first broadbill seen in New Zealand waters weighing 400 pounds, he gave the great impetus to big game fishing as a sport. Since then other records have been established: a 1000-pound mako shark, a 976-pound black marlin, and a 922-pound thresher shark are among them. Offshore fishing yields an assorted bag as well as an abundance; as many as fifty different species have been taken from the Bay of Plenty. The warm water that sweeps along mile upon mile of snow-white beaches brings fish that follow the smaller, edible sea creatures, so that the surfcaster also is assured of a fine catch.

During weekends families leave their baches to catch fish by netting. Equipped with two rowboats and a long, light net, they work as a team by rowing out with the net stretched between the two boats, then hauling it, filled with wriggling fish, into a beach. The catch is usually the silver-bellied snappers whose frantic leaps expose their thick-lipped drooping mouths. When the catch is sorted the smaller fish are tossed back into the sea; the rest are cleaned and packed away in freezers. Where high, powerful waves roll in to crash on sandy beaches, surfboard riders balance for a quarter mile or so as they speed toward land in the curl of a comber. Other water lovers ski in the wake of speedboats across lakes and quiet inlets. Skin diving has its legion of followers also. Adept divers snatch crayfish from between underwater rocks, and scallops and *pauas* (abalones) abound in shallow water for the taking.

Auckland's anniversary, January 29, marks the greatest one-day midsummer regatta in the world. Whatever the weather, Auckland takes to the sail. Never fewer than five hundred craft, from great keelers down to one-boy seven-footers, participate in the races. With the sound of the starter's gun big yachts race to the gulf and back and the winner's prize is the Heather Cup. The little ones tack and tip over while their occupants yell; hundreds of power boats follow the racing craft and thousands of spectators, lining the shores, wave and shout their enthusiasm. Anniversary Day is a big time for sail-minded Aucklanders— a colorful day with the white and multicolored sails shimmering against Auckland's blue harbor.

Sailing picnickers at a popular beach near Wellington.

However, shore and water attractions pale before the interest shown in horses, especially fast horses. This interest probably stems from pride, for New Zealand stud farms produce thoroughbreds of the highest quality which are often bought by overseas trainers to achieve, eventually, international fame. Again, credit is given to New Zealand grasses and mild climate for building stamina in foals from imported mares that is unequaled anywhere. As a result of this interest in horses, racing and trotting are by far the most popular spectator sports. In one year, 380 race meetings are held in New Zealand. Even the smallest towns have race tracks, which are closed on Sundays, Christmas, and Easter only. The larger cities support magnificent courses with luxuriant gardens spread about their wide grandstands. Race meetings attract thousands of people who regard them as social occasions; in smaller centers a picnic atmosphere prevails. Attention is focused on betting, also. It was a New Zealander, G. A. Julius, who invented the totalizator, or tote, now in world-wide use. New Zealanders wager about $150,000,000 annually on their favorite horses.

In competitive sports rowing, golf, tennis, hockey, cricket, and softball have their place but none of these will ever share the popularity of the national game, rugby football of amateur status. A tough, rough game, played to rigid rules, rugby and its all-star team, the All-Blacks (so named for their black uniforms), produce more universal excitement throughout New Zealand than baseball's World Series does in the U.S.A.

During the winter months every lot and field is cleared for rugby practice. Up go the goal posts and out come the young school players. A team is comprised of fifteen players, including a captain. After a thorough check for uniform correctness, deportment, and faults in footwear likely to wound, the teams march out to the field led by their captains. In turn the captains call for cheers for the opponents, each team dances a soul-stirring *haka,* the referee tosses a coin and the game commences. Boys start learning rugby at the age of seven; they learn the science of the dive pass, getting down in the scrum (huddle), and the multi-ruled problems of obtaining possession when the ball is put in on the tight head side of the scrum. During the game fair play is observed keenly and when it is over, although begrimed and often bloodied, the losers are taught to keep a stiff upper lip. A lack of punctuality, dirty boots and other attire, improper behavior (such as losing one's temper), unfair tactics, poor sportsmanship, disloyalty to the coach, talking out of turn, too much individualism, or not knowing the rules can hinder a boy's progress to a higher status no matter how good his over-all game. Such is the training for young aspirants to the All-Blacks, famous throughout the world since the turn of the century for their mettle on the rugby field.

New Zealand athletes are renowned for their records at the Olympic Games. One great runner, Jack Lovelock, won the 1500-meter race in 1936, setting a record that stood until 1952. Yvette Williams, at the Helsinki Olympics, won the women's broad jump and in 1954 three gold medals at the British Empire Games in Vancouver. Murray Halberg's times over two, three, and four miles are the fastest in world track history, while he holds the second best at 5000 meters. His best times over distances ranging from 1500 meters to the marathon and his unbeaten record in international races over two and three miles assure him a place among the greatest runners of all time. His best times are: 1500 meters, 3 minutes, 38.8 seconds; one mile, 3 minutes, 57.5 seconds; two miles, 8 minutes, 30 seconds; three miles, 13 minutes, 13.10 seconds; and his marathon, 2 hours, 28 minutes, and 43 seconds.

In 1962, Murray Halberg's club mate, Peter Snell, broke the 800-meter and 880-yard world records with times of 1 minute, 44.3 seconds; 1 minute, 45.1 seconds; and, for one mile, 3 minutes, 54.4 seconds. In early 1962 New Zealand runners held all the world records.

Robert Charles, the left-handed golf player and former New Zealand open golf champion, won the British open golf championship in 1963. New Zealand's open-air life and its outdoor activities pay off in the results shown by her athletic champions.

16

/\.\/\.\/\.\/\.\/\.\

Famous New Zealanders

SIR EDMUND HILLARY exemplifies the benefits of an outdoor environment that builds fortitude and vigor in addition to daring and tenacity. In 1953, when the news of his and Tenzing's epic achievement in reaching Mount Everest's 29,141-foot peak was flashed around the world, Hillary had behind him fifteen years of mountaineering experience in New Zealand and in the Swiss and Austrian Alps.

It was by chance that Hillary became a mountain climber, for after two years at the University of Auckland he settled down in what he expected was to be his life work, bee-keeping. His father, an apiarist near Auckland, was his employer. But when Hillary was twenty and vacationing in the Southern Alps he looked up and saw Mount Cook for the first time. He saw and

Sir Edmund Hillary

vowed to conquer that majestic Cloud Piercer. Hillary studied the technicalities of mountain climbing and during World War II, while in training for the Air Force near Mount Egmont, he snatched every opportunity for practice. Enforced hospitalization, while on active service, was more irksome as an interruption to his chosen career than were his wounds. After the war Hillary accomplished several outstanding climbs, the most notable being the ascent of Mount Cook along the south ridge, a treacherous stretch of ice and rock never before (or since) attempted.

The climb that culminated in the conquest of Mount Everest started from the southern end of the mountain at an elevation of 28,000 feet, the highest ever attained over thirty-two years by eight separate expeditions. This was the "invisible barrier" level that had always thwarted previous climbers. But at six-thirty on the morning of May 29 Hillary and Tenzing stepped out of their tent and, in Hillary's words, "We strapped on our crampons and tied on our nylon rope, grasped our ice-axes and were ready to go."

The two men crossed the south summit and reached the ridge leading to the main summit—a sheer rock precipice towering above their heads. It appeared, at first, to be unsurmountable, but the intrepid climbers found a narrow gap between the rock wall and a great oval mass of overhanging ice. With the possibility that the ice cornice would collapse, they cautiously levered their way upward, inch by inch. From the top they saw enormous ice cliffs, alternating with steep snow slopes, ahead of them. By thrusting with his ice ax Hillary ascertained that everything was solid and firm as they toiled onward, then, "A few more whacks of the ice-axe, a few more weary steps and we were on the summit of Everest." It had taken five and a half hours to climb a thousand feet.

Since Mount Everest's conquest Edmund Hillary has led other expeditions to the Himalayas and headed the New Zealand Support Party in the Commonwealth Transantarctic Expedition. The Explorers' Club of New York and other clubs in America and Europe have honored him. He has also become a man of letters: his Himalayan experiences became an exciting book called *High Adventure.*

Among New Zealand writers Katherine Mansfield undoubtedly ranks highest. The originality of her prose, its depth in human concepts, and her talent in creating a mood with clarity yet briefness captured world attention before reaching the land of her birth, New Zealand. She was born Katherine Beauchamp in Wellington, in 1888, the third of five children. Her father, Harold Beauchamp, belonged to the first generation of New

Zealand-born pioneers; he was later knighted for distinguished public service. As a family the Beauchamps were solid, practical nation builders. Katherine, the introspective, sensitive girl, was a misfit. She decided to become a writer when in boarding school in London and, after several experiments, took her grandmother's name as a nom de plume. Back in her beloved homeland Katherine failed to conform as society then expected so, after repeated breaches with that provincial way of life, she left Wellington in 1908, never to return. Yet Katherine Mansfield's choicest stories, always touched with nostalgia for the land she loved, stem from childhood memories. Her last link with home was her only brother Leslie, who stayed with her in London. It was the year 1915 and, as a soldier, he was on his way to the battle front. Homesick together, they planned to return to New Zealand after the war. But Leslie was killed near Armentières soon afterward and his sister, stunned by this loss, infused her writing even more strongly with poignancy. Some years later Katherine Mansfield wrote a tribute to Leslie Beauchamp.

To L. H. B. (1894-1915)

Last night for the first time since you were dead
I walked with you, my brother, in a dream.
We were at home again beside the stream
Fringed with tall berry bushes, white and red. . . .

Katherine Mansfield's last years were lived in France, but the memory of beautiful New Zealand remained and affected her writing until she died, a victim of tuberculosis, in 1923. New Zealand has awakened to the realization of her extraordinary talent, for a memorial now stands in her honor close to where she lived as a girl in Wellington.

Sylvia Ashton-Warner, a contemporary New Zealand writer, guides little Maori children through the early intricate stages of learning. But like Katherine Mansfield, she too has come abroad for recognition. The first of her successful books was published in the United States in 1959. Her more recent book, *Teacher,* explains her method of encouraging pupils in finding expression from within themselves rather than having it imposed upon them. Sylvia Ashton-Warner describes her system as a Creative Teaching Scheme.

Another New Zealander who is contributing to the arts and who receives world attention is Ngaio Marsh, expert mystery writer. And the late Sir David Low started his famous career as a cartoonist before leaving New Zealand, his homeland.

New Zealand's countryside inspired an earlier writer, Samuel Butler, to produce his masterpiece, *Erewhon,* regarded as one of the great classics of the English language. Filled with subtlety and humor, *Erewhon's* utopian setting is the mountain-rimmed valley where Samuel Butler, an English immigrant, bought land in 1860 for sheep raising. He had rebelled against the pious, bigoted atmosphere in which he had grown up, persuading his father, a clergyman, to finance his trip to New Zealand. In less than five years, when he sold his thriving farm, Butler had doubled the $20,000 his father had grudgingly given him. Although at first his home on the Canterbury Plains was a sod hut, Butler had a grand piano hauled in by bullock team, for in addition to being a writer and a sheep farmer he was also an accomplished pianist. As he practiced Handel's music in the grandeur of his farm's setting he conceived the idea for the satirical novel that he later wrote in England.

New Zealanders are proud that one of their most distinguished citizens was of Maori origin. Among his other accomplishments he, too, was a writer of note. His Maori name was Te Rangi Hiroa, but to admirers in countries beyond New Zealand shores and to those who were privileged to work with him, he was Sir Peter Buck, K.C.M.G., D.S.O., M.A., Litt.D., D.Sc., M.D., Ch.B. One of his books, *Vikings of the Sunrise,* published in 1938, was widely read in America.

Sir Peter Buck was born in 1880 and spent his boyhood in Maori country north of Taranaki. He won a scholarship to a Maori college and another to the University of Otago, where he obtained his M.D. degree. During World War I, Sir Peter saw overseas service as a medical officer for which he was decorated with the Distinguished Service Order. Later he was professor of anthropology at Yale University before accepting the directorship of the Museum of Polynesian Antiquities in Honolulu. When Sir Peter died in 1951, after a long and fruitful life, a memorial taking the form of an early Maori canoe was raised to his honor in Maori country.

Sir Ernest Rutherford, Baron Rutherford of Nelson, goes

Sir Peter Buck, at a reception given in his honor in 1949.

down in history as one of the greatest scientists of his day. His basic studies established the existence and nature of radioactive transformations, the electrical structure of matter, and the nuclear nature of the atom. Ernest Rutherford started life in 1871 in Nelson where, as one of twelve children, he helped on the farm and in his father's carriage-building business. The young Ernest won scholarships providing education, first at a private school, then the Canterbury University College, and finally, when he was twenty-five, at Trinity College, Cambridge. After holding professorships at several prominent universities he became president of the British Association first, then of the Royal Society. Many British and foreign degrees, including the Nobel prize for chemistry in 1908, were bestowed upon Lord Rutherford. He was knighted in 1914 and created a baron in 1931. This unassuming, modest man, who dedicated his life to science, died in 1937 at Cambridge, England.

Richard Cockburn Maclaurin, a contemporary of Lord Rutherford's, was brought from Scotland to New Zealand as a child. His talents lay in mathematics and law. After finishing his education at Cambridge, he returned to New Zealand as professor of mathematics at Wellington's university; then he was drawn to the U.S.A., when his outstanding administrative abilities were recognized, to become president of Massachusetts Institute of Technology. Dr. Maclaurin was born in 1870 and died in 1920.

New Zealanders in the practice of medicine, anthropology, and ethnology have found recognition in countries outside their own. These achievements of a young nation comparatively small in population are understandable, for the staunch pioneers endowed their descendants with some of their own vast energy and determination to succeed.

17

/\/\/\/\/\

New Zealand's Place in Today's World

TODAY, although New Zealanders are obliged to register at the polls, they are not compelled to vote. However, only the direst circumstances will keep a voter from exercising the privilege of having a say in the government of his country. This tremendous interest in government applies to New Zealand's Maori population as much as it does to its Pakehas.

New Zealand, which attained dominion status in 1907, is a self-governing member of the British Commonwealth of Nations. It is a constitutional monarchy whose government is based on British constitutional principles and the head of state is Britain's reigning monarch—currently, Queen Elizabeth II. Parliament consists of a House of Representatives comprised of eighty members who are elected for a maximum term of three years. The Governor-General, representing the British Crown, is government's formal executive head. He is appointed for a five-year term by the Queen, after consultation with and the approval of the New Zealand Government.

There are two main parties in New Zealand—National and Labor. At any general election these parties, other political parties, and those who stand as independents state their policies before the electors. The Communist party contests a few seats, but it has never had a member elected. From 1935 until 1949 the Labor party was in power, making its prime objective the preservation of New Zealand's standard of living, which had been threatened by adverse market trends as a result of the depression in the 1930s. The National party won the election in 1949, holding sway until 1957 when Labor again took the helm. But in 1960 the National party, the more conservative of the two, returned to power with the Right Honorable Keith Holyoake as Prime Minister.

After a general election the leader of the winning party, the Prime Minister, is asked by the Governor-General to choose members for an Executive Council. Then the official acts of the Governor-General are performed only on the advice of this body. The leader of the defeated party becomes the Leader of the Opposition.

With slight amendments, New Zealand law is also based upon British law. It is administered by ministers of the Crown and official appointments are on a permanent basis regardless of which party is in power.

Government controls many projects that in other countries are the concern of private enterprise. It owns insurance companies and tourist agencies, the postal system and Post Office

Savings Banks, trading banks, trustee offices, and employment agencies. Almost all transportation, whether railroad, bus, or air, is government-owned, as are radio stations to which the listener pays an annual fee before he may tune in. Interest in the welfare of the individual is seen in the excellent educational services, in provision for old age and the disabled, and in a high minimum wage. Under a Social Security program hospital and a wide range of medical care is provided free by the government. Patients who choose to enter private hospitals or consult their own doctors do so at a reduced rate, for private hospitals and doctors are subsidized. District nurses employed by the Department of Health visit the homes of convalescent patients and the elderly; they pay periodic visits to schools and clinics where they also assist with vaccinations and inoculations. School children receive free dental services and instruction in dental hygiene. The Department of Health also keeps a close watch on the processing and sale of foods, which must pass rigid tests before being offered for sale. Food samples are analyzed in the Dominion Laboratory, for food laws ban the use of chemical preservatives, a rule that applies to imported foods also.

State aid is given to one voluntary organization that contributes to New Zealand's low infant mortality rate of 20 for every 1000 live births, exclusive of the Maoris. This is the Royal New Zealand Society for the Health of Women and Children. Commonly called the Plunket Society, it was named for the wife of the Governor-General who played a large part in the society's formation in 1907. Sir Truby King, a doctor who was inspired to "help the mothers and save the babies," established day clinics, Karitane (a training center for nurses), and hospitals for sick children. Today, few towns and villages are without Plunket Centers where the system's principles of regularity in feeding are practiced and taught to prospective mothers. And few mothers omit the weekly visit to the clinic for their babies' weighing and health checkups.

Other private enterprises that operate in the interests of New Zealand's citizens are subsidized by government. The financial resources of the Society for the Protection of Women and Children are augmented by government subsidy. The society works in co-operation with the Child Welfare Department when cases of cruelty or neglect are brought to light. Lawyers are made available if a court case or legal advise is necessary. This society is an international enterprise that exchanges correspondence and gifts with other rural women's organizations throughout the world, such as the New England Farm and Garden Association in the United States. Several years ago an awareness of the plight of farm women in lonely, remote areas caused the formation of the Women's Division of Federated Farmers. Government again springs into action with a subsidy to the wages of "emergency housekeepers" who move in for periods up to four weeks, or longer if necessary, when the mother of a household is ill or is advised to rest in one of the five homes maintained by the society. The Women's Division of Federated Farmers brings solace to country-dwelling women in time of stress and acts as their voice in matters of national importance.

Under Social Security, pensions are paid to widows, orphans, invalids, and those temporarily incapacitated. Pensions are available, also, to the unemployed, although since the depression of the 1930s unemployment has been practically non-existent in New Zealand. Family benefits include a weekly subsidy to the mother of every child up to sixteen years of age and eighteen if the child remains in school until that age. Schooling is free from kindergarten to college level and attendance is compulsory between the ages of seven and fifteen. Grade schools are co-educational but in most high schools the boys and girls are separated. Education is taken to children who live in far-removed areas, by means of a Correspondence School that also provides technical courses for adults. Scholarships allow country children to attend boarding schools. Government helps pay for transportation in more inaccessible areas, even a horseback allowance if a child rides to school. Universities and agricultural colleges charge tuition fees, but when a student passes the university entrance examination and completes his first year these fees are repaid by government. And if attending one of the five special colleges for teacher training, dental nursing, and other health services, students are paid a salary as they learn.

In teaching, during recent years, greater emphasis has been placed on physical education, teacher aids, social studies, and the arts—particularly music. The Education Department's duties embrace a wide field of activities. It gives advice on vocational guidance, special training for the handicapped and the exceptionally talented student; it cares for the underprivileged and delinquent child. The department recognizes the importance of well-qualified instructors, so a high standard has been stressed in the teacher-training colleges. Through direct observation of young children, through lectures, field trips, and individual conferences, future teachers learn to translate theory into actual teaching experience. Upon graduation the new teacher is given a Diploma in Education and is launched on a rewarding career, well prepared and confident.

Each of the four main universities receives grants from the National Council; each offers courses in the arts, science, commerce, and law, but each places emphasis on certain specialties. Auckland's University College specializes in architecture, Wellington's Victoria University College emphasizes its law department, Christchurch's Canterbury University College stresses engineering and art, and the University of Otago, near Dunedin, has departments of medicine, dentistry, mines, social science, and physical education. In addition to its four universities, government sponsors many technical and agricultural colleges which include, in their wide curricula, animal husbandry, agronomy, soil constituents, plant diseases, and subjects that provide a means of boosting New Zealand's secondary industries.

In May 1962, New Zealand's Prime Minister, the Right Honorable Keith Holyoake, welcomed the one thousandth Asian student to come to New Zealand under the Colombo Plan. In part he said, "This policy . . . not only has importance for the economic development of Asian countries but helps to build up good will and understanding." The Colombo Plan for Cooperative Economic Development in South and Southeast Asia was started by British Commonwealth countries to eliminate the tensions that are the cause of war. Also, and mainly, it was the result of a genuine impulse to help the underprivileged peoples of other countries. Under the Colombo Plan aid program, Asian students are brought to New Zealand's schools and universities to train in a wide variety of subjects which include agriculture, government administration, and English language teaching. An important feature of the Colombo Plan is the assistance given in the economic development of Southeast Asian countries. Experts have been sent overseas—to Pakistan to help with irrigation projects and to Ceylon for farming research, among other assignments.

Under the Fulbright plan there is an exchange of students with the United States. Both research students and men and women of high academic standing have gone to New Zealand to teach or to study. This exchange of citizens with other countries has created an awareness among New Zealanders of other countries and their people.

New Zealand gives full support to the United Nations and since 1954 has occupied a seat as an elected member of the Security Council. Her delegates recognize the United Nations Organization as an upholder of collective security and as an instrument in spreading beneficial work through its specialized agencies. New Zealand participates in all of these agencies (except the International Bank and the International Monetary Fund) by providing experienced officials to their management. The government and the New Zealand people have contributed $5,000,000, or more, to the United Nations International Children's Emergency Fund.

In 1951 New Zealand entered the Tripartite Security Treaty with Australia and the United States. This treaty is known as the Anzus Pact; it exists, basically, as an aid in the economic development and stability of countries in the Pacific region. The three countries involved regard the Anzus Pact as a necessary partnership, in a new era, between advanced and undeveloped nations. The treaty aims at strengthening peace by mutual action in accordance with the principles of the United Nations Charter.

On May 8 and 9, 1962, the Anzus Council held their periodic meeting in Canberra, Australia. The Honorable Sir Garfield

Barwick, Minister for External Affairs, represented Australia; the Right Honorable K. J. Holyoake, Prime Minister and Minister of External Affairs, represented New Zealand; the Honorable Dean Rusk, Secretary of State, represented the United States.

The conferring ministers reaffirmed their governments' undertaking under the Charter of the United Nations to preserve world peace. They expressed concern that, despite this obligation, accepted by all U.N. members, peace was threatened in Southeast Asia. However, they decided to continue with plans for the economic and social welfare of the small countries in Southeast Asia, with the goal of bringing them to a point of development where they could choose for themselves their future form of government and international relationships. The meeting in Canberra was successful in strengthening, still further, the friendly co-operation between the three Anzus member countries. Then Mr. Rusk flew on to New Zealand; he was the first Secretary of State of the United States to visit the country while in office.

Although Mr. Rusk's visit to Australia and New Zealand was primarily for the Anzus meeting, he found these Commonwealth countries anxiously preoccupied with an emergency that threatened their economic future. Great Britain was seeking membership in the European Economic Community—the Common Market. Mr. Holyoake had already issued a protesting statement, couched in strong words, just prior to the Canberra meeting:

"The whole basis of New Zealand economy—built on selling in the British market—is at stake. . . . We are fighting for our very livelihood because 91% of our exported butter, 94% of our cheese and 94% of our mutton and lamb is sold in the

British market. . . . I want our people to know that in these critical negotiations New Zealand is fighting tooth and nail to protect our vital trading rights and interests in the British market. . . . If Britain were to join the Common Market without adequate safeguards for us—with the abolition of preference and the application of tariffs, levies, minimum prices and other restrictions against our dairy produce and meat on the British market—New Zealand's overseas earnings would be slashed by many millions of pounds."

While in New Zealand Mr. Rusk expressed his opposing views on the emergency at a state dinner in Wellington. He pleaded for the American concept of "open trading arrangements," reduction of tariff barriers, and global arrangements for cereals and other key commodities. "A more open trading world," he said, "seemed to the United States a far better approach than permanent maintenance of preferential systems. . . . Now, Great Britain seeks Common Market membership. We did not urge it. But when the British asked us as old friends for our views, we responded favorably. . . . We share with Britain the judgment that she can better maintain her strength inside the Common Market than outside it."

Mr. Rusk suggested one new outlet for New Zealand primary produce. "We think there is opportunity for collective international action among all agricultural producing nations to explore new techniques for making this rich bounty available for the welfare of the less developed countries." Mr. Rusk also predicted that the United States was a growing market for New Zealand. "We think that we can demonstrate in the months ahead that we have a strong interest in your prosperity. We have common interests. We are buying more from you than you are from us but we will get around that in due course. We expect to be a growing market for you and hope you will be for us."

Over several days the *New Zealand Herald* published various editorials concerning Mr. Rusk's visit. One of them said, in part:

"The fact is that Mr. Rusk has had to argue a difficult brief —that the preferential system, on which Australia and New Zealand have based so much of their economic development, should be scrapped in favor of open multilateral trade. . . . In making such a change New Zealand must not only cope with a major switch in markets, but must also face the high agricultural protectionism against efficient producers which survives unabated in arrangements like the European Economic Community."

At a crucial meeting in London and at another in Brussels, Australian and New Zealand representatives strongly criticized Britain's agreement with the Common Market to end imperial preferential duty-free, unrestricted entry for almost all Commonwealth products by 1970 if she joined the group. Both countries would face drastic consequences if Britain were to enter the Common Market without first providing adequate safeguards to their trading interests in respect to the British market. But as one New Zealand spokesman said, "We understand the wish of Great Britain to join the Community both on political and economic grounds. We believe too that the Six want to see Britain a member. If that is to be achieved the gulf which at present divides the parties to the negotiations will have to be bridged. The bridge will have to be built from both sides. The bridge will have to be big enough to carry the vital interests of Commonwealth trade."

*Parliament Buildings, Wellington. Statue at right is that of John Bal-
lance, Prime Minister of New Zealand from 1891 to 1893.*

Discussions continue between the six Common Market members, Great Britain, and her Commonwealth nations. It is possible that they will continue for a long time into the future, perhaps for many months—or years. In the meantime New Zealanders are making preparations to face drastic changes in their
economic security if it becomes necessary; their thoughts are
turning to manufacturing and to the seeking of new markets

nearer home. They will overcome adversity as they have met and overcome every crisis in the past.

Queen Elizabeth spoke truly, at the end of her recent visit to New Zealand's people: "The impression that we have received is of a great and united people . . . and that to your united strength is constantly being added the vitality and skill of settlers from many countries of the Old World. May this concord of races flourish in the fruitful land and in the splendid and healthy climate which Providence has given you."

Index